# Mastering Your Hidden Self

# About the Author

**SERGE KAHILI KING**, Ph.D., has been actively engaged in the fields of parapsychology, paraphysics, bioenergetics, and social technology for more than twenty years. His studies have taken him to many parts of the world, including most of North and South America, Europe, and Africa. During seven years in West Africa he conducted an in-depth study of the magicoreligious systems, while at the same time carrying out broad programs of socioeconomic development. For his latter work he received a medal from the President of Senegal.

Besides Quest books *Imagineering, Kahuna Healing,* and *Earth Energies,* Dr. King has authored *Mana Physics, The Hidden Knowledge of Huna Science,* and *The Pyramid Energy Handbook,* and many articles, courses, and lectures in all his fields of endeavor. A member of Phi Beta Kappa, he holds a Masters and Ph.D. degree and has knowledge of eight languages.

Initiated by his father into an esoteric order of kahunas at the age of fourteen, Dr. King has studied under some of the finest masters of psychospiritual knowledge from Africa to Hawaii. He directs the activities of the Order of Huna International. An ex-Marine, he lives in Princeville, HI, with his wife and three children and is engaged in research, teaching, counseling, and healing.

# Mastering Your Hidden Self

## A Guide to the HUNA WAY

### Serge King

A publication supported by
THE KERN FOUNDATION

## Quest Books
Theosophical Publishing House

Wheaton, Illinois ♦ Chennai (Madras), India

Quest Books
Theosophical Publishing House
P. O. Box 270
Wheaton, IL 60187-0270

www.questbooks.net


Library of Congress Cataloging-in-Publication Data

King, Serge.
Mastering your hidden self.
(A Quest Book)
"A Quest original."
Includes index.
1. Occult sciences.    I. Title.
BF1999.K49    1985    133    84-40509
ISBN 978-0-8356-0591-5

Printed in the United States of America

This book is dedicated to Gloria Dawn Denkhaus, my best student, my best friend, and my wife.

# Acknowledgments

Acknowledgments are due to all my students whose
feedback enabled me to keep refining this material; to
Jane Roberts and Barry Kaufman, from whose books
I borrowed certain phrases to explain the Huna knowledge; to my editor, Shirley Nicholson, whose good
advice helped to stabilize the theme of the book;
and finally to my typewriter, Fred, whose persistent
good will kept the manuscript flowing.

# Contents

# Contents

# Preface

Since my last book, *Kahuna Healing*, many people
have asked me about practical applications of Huna insight into the nature of the self, which is the reason
for bringing out the present book. They have also asked
me about my own training as a kahuna. Since this has
a great deal of bearing on your use of this book, I'd like to
"talk story" a bit on that subject.

In my life so far I've experienced many different
forms of training, including school and college, post-
graduate studies, the military, special language and
technical courses, and others. In my opinion, kahuna
training was the hardest of all. Perhaps I can explain that
better by relating a few incidents of such training.

My father was my toughest teacher. Before I understood what kahuna training was all about, I harbored a lot
of resentment toward him for certain things he did.
One occasion that stands out in my memory took place
when I was fifteen. We were building a house, working in the basement, and he told me to get him an awl. I

had never heard of an awl, so I asked him what it was. He simply said, "Just go get one." Well, instead of applying anything I had learned the previous year about intuition and awareness, I got mad at how "unfair" he was. I blocked my mind to everything but my anger, and of course found nothing even resembling an awl. After a few more wasted trips and mounting resentment on my part, he went and got the thing himself.

You could say he should have described an awl to me so I could have found it and learned what it was. But the lesson had nothing to do with awls. Nor did it have to do specifically with using my extended awareness to intuit what an awl was or to pick it out of a tool box. If that were the case, my father would have said, as he had on many other occasions, "Use your mind." No, the lesson in this case was about initiative. I knew how to be more observant in the present moment, which would have included being aware of what my father was working on and what would be logically necessary or useful to enable him to continue (e.g., "something to make a hole with"), and I knew how to let my mind bring images according to my intent and how to let my subconscious lead me toward things I might be looking for. What my father did was to give me an opportunity to use what I knew. What I did, in that instance, was to put my energy and talent into feeling sorry for myself.

In Africa once, a few days after my mentor, M'Bala, had guided me through a particularly powerful experience of "becoming" a leopard, he handed me a kind of large, stone bead, without saying anything. "What's this?" I asked. "A stone," he replied. "I can see that," I said, "but what's it for? Is it an amulet?" "It could be used for one," he said, indifferently. Feeling a little frustrated, I asked, "Well, what am I supposed to do with it?" "Anything you like," was his answer. So I just thanked him for it with a shrug and put it in my pocket. In all the rest of the time I spent with him, M'Bala never referred to the stone again. It wasn't until five

years later, back in the States, that it occurred to me
to apply the knowledge of the leopard experience for
tuning in to the stone. Doing something with it was
entirely up to me.

Fortunately, I wasn't that dense during all my lessons.
By the time I started working with my Hawaiian
"uncle," Wana Kahili, I was doing a lot better. He would
suggest a practice, and I would do it and extend it as
far as I could and tell him my results; he would suggest re-
finements or further extensions, and I would follow
those and add inventions of my own; he would either
guide me further in that direction or suggest a new one.
As long as I kept moving, he would keep teaching
and I would keep learning. If I failed to follow up on anything, it was simply dropped and never mentioned
again, until and if I did something with it. For the
kahunas, self-development means that responsibility for
your development lies with yourself. There is no limit
as to how far you can go, and there will always be a guide
of some kind available at every stage. But each person
has to get there on his or her own two feet. There is no one
to push you or pull you, coax or cajole you, force you or
lead you along. And that's why it's tough.

This book is like that. In here is knowledge that
can effectively transform your life . . . if you use it. And
once you've tried it and experimented with it, there
will be even more to learn. But just owning this book,
reading it, and storing it on a shelf won't do much for you
and won't open the doors to greater adventures that
lie ahead and all around you.

Initiative is the hardest and most important lesson
of all.

# Introduction:
## THE REDISCOVERY OF HUNA

Anyone who uses his eyes to see and his ears to hear
must come to the conclusion that our world and the
entire universe operate on some very basic principles.*
Some very few enlightened people have, from time to
time, discovered all or part of these principles and
have attempted to present them to the rest of humanity.
Invariably, however, the simple principles they ex-
pounded were expanded, padded, and distorted by the
less enlightened ones who came after them. The
Buddha outlined eight clear steps to self-realization, but
Buddhism became one of the most elaborately ritualized
religions the world has ever seen, and the simple
teaching was almost forgotten in the process. Moses
presented ten commandments to the Hebrews, and an
immensely complicated religion was the result. Jesus re-
duced the whole of the Law to two commandments,

---

*The masculine pronouns *he, him* and *his* are used for convenience and are understood to include women.

1

and the vast, world-wide complex of Christianity grew out of it. Mohammed channeled the Koran and developed a simple and straightforward religion based on the acknowledgment of God and five prayers a day, but to that was added the highly detailed codification of Islamic law. It is as if a man were given a clear blueprint for happiness and then purposely blinded himself so that he would have to find his way by trial and error.

## SECRET TEACHINGS

In addition to the outer teachings of the great religious leaders, it has long been held by thoughtful persons that secret teachings were passed on from teacher to close disciple, teachings that revealed the true nature of God and the universe. Lao Tse carefully veiled the real meaning of his teaching in *The Way Of Life* (*Tao Te Ching*) by using language so simple that it could be interpreted in many different ways, and the Chinese author of *The Secret Of The Golden Flower* did a similar thing, using the technique of allegory. Bodhidharma is supposed to have brought the secret teachings of Buddha into China. The school he developed was Ch'an Buddhism, which later became Zen Buddhism in Japan. Far earlier, the secret teachings of Yoga were brought together by Patanjali in his Aphorisms, and much later the Sufis claimed to hold the secret teachings of Islam. Secret teachings are supposed to be contained in the early Hebrew writings, as well as in the language of the Old Testament itself, and the early Christian writers of the Gospels made it clear that the outer meaning of what they wrote was not the whole of what they had to say. Several times Jesus states that he will explain to the disciples in secret the meaning of the parables, and he even tells the crowds that his meaning will be clear only to those able to understand. To add further to the mysteries, tales are still told of hidden Tibetan monasteries where the secrets of life are contained, and secret societies

like the Rosicrucians continue to claim possession of un-
told truths. But even obvious facts can seem like
secrets to those who are not trained to see them.

## New Hope

One thing that binds most religions together is a
belief in the spiritual nature of man. But unfortunately
this nature is all too often thought of as tainted, if not
evil. Even when that is not the case, the spiritual is
emphasized to the detriment of the physical. Not only
that, but those not of the same religion or religious
practice are considered more evil and unworthy. The
result of all this is either a desire to escape from reality
while still living in the physical world, or a tendency
to ignore or degrade the physical by directing the
attention to the goal of ultimate happiness in a future,
spiritual world. And from this has come general misery,
bloody wars, and little hope for happiness on earth.

At a certain point new possibilities appeared on
the horizon: science and technology on the one hand,
sociology and psychology on the other. Together
they would change the earth and make it a better and
happier place in which to live. However, the byproduct
was a complete disbelief in the spiritual nature of man
and a concerted attempt to bend inanimate nature
to man's will by whatever means seem necessary. For the
great majority of scientists, technicians, sociologists,
and psychologists, man is a physical being only, a
random conglomeration of chemicals and machinery
that tends to break down a lot and needs to be carefully
monitored and controlled. Furthermore, their belief
is that both man and nature are subject only to physical
laws, that these laws are already known. Whenever
they run up against something inexplicable in their
accepted physical terms, they either ignore it, pronounce
it a fraud, construct absurdly complex physical
explanations which are no more than wild guesses,
or try to destroy it. And from this has come general

misery, bloody wars, and little hope of happiness on earth.

In desperation, because of the failures of traditional religion and modern science, people are resurrecting medieval practices such as witchcraft and various forms of occultism that promise the individual control over his or her environment. These practices contain elements of truth and can be either fun or dangerous, but the results are usually haphazard. Another path being taken is that of positive thinking and its derivatives, which contain much good, but they are limited to personal transformation, and their results are also haphazard. Finally, of course, there is the drug culture, but this is escapism pure and simple, and the results are nearly always disastrous.

Into all this darkness comes the shining light of Huna. It is religious in the sense that it inspires man to attain spiritual perfection. It is scientific because it deals with the physical here and now and its techniques produce repeatable effects on people and the environment. Huna is a philosophy of life with a strong but simple code of ethics. Some consider it to be occult because it works with forces that are unseen but very real. It is all embracing because every religion contains parts of it and science is beginning to recognize its principles in the workings of the universe.

### AN ANCIENT TEACHING

Let me make it clear that Huna is *not* identical with the traditional religion of Hawaii, and my comments do not concern that religion in its objective, historical form. Rather, I am presenting an older, more universal Way, which I will illustrate through Hawaiian terms and concepts.

Huna is incredibly old, probably as old as the creation of man himself. Legend traces Huna back to Mu and later Atlantis, but the first historical indication we have of its presence is in ancient Egypt. According to the kahunas, sometime in the millennia before Christ a group of initiates got together and created an artificial language by means of which the knowledge of Huna could be communicated from generation to generation. This secret language formed the roots of another language which could be used openly, so that no matter how the outer language was used and what beliefs were constructed with it, the root knowledge would remain like a well-preserved secret. Many symbolic meanings were added to the basic secret meanings, and meanings were often duplicated in several roots to further ensure the survival of the knowledge. There is some anthropological evidence to support the kahuna belief that this language and the knowledge it contained spread from the Pacific throughout the rest of the world, and traces of it still exist in many ancient place names.

Now all of this might sound as fanciful as the claims of certain secret societies which pretend to an unbroken line of knowledge, tracing their origin to ancient times, *were it not for the fact that the code to the secret language of Huna has been rediscovered!* The evidence is available to anyone who cares to read it. After years of studying the sources, I am convinced that Huna did indeed spread out from Polynesia.

### A TRIBUTE TO MAX LONG

The man who first revealed the Huna code to the West was Max Freedom Long, a student of psychology, teacher for many years in Hawaii, and a one-time member of the Theosophy movement. From the beginning of his stay in the islands, Long was fascinated with the powers of the kahunas, who were the native medicine men and shamans of Polynesia. They had techniques of healing people and controlling the environment that actually worked, but they weren't about to reveal their methods to a nonkahuna. During his many years of residence there Long tried to discover the secret, but in spite of the fact that he was witness to many seeming miracles performed by the kahunas and was even benefited by some, he was unable to discover the secret on Hawaiian soil. It was five years after he had left Hawaii that Long woke up in the middle of the night with a possible answer to the riddle. The kahunas had to have some way of transmitting their lore to their successors. Perhaps the secret could be found within the language itself.

The inspiration paid off, but not without more years of hard work. By correlating the known Hawaiian traditions about magic and psychological therapy used by the kahunas on their patients; the Western science of psychology; occult lore; and the root meanings of certain key Hawaiian words, Long was at last able to piece together the main elements of a scientific, psycho-religious system which he called *Huna* (*ka-huna* means "the secret"). Long formed an organization called Huna Research Associates to study the system, and several books were published which detailed the results of the investigation. Most significantly, it was found that the principles of Huna not only provided a logical and consistent explanation of human psychology, but when applied they produced solid results. Beyond that, the principles provided the same consistent and logical basis for what many have termed magic, and which today falls under the rubric of para-psychology. Psychic abilities such as telepathy, clairvoyance and mind over matter were no longer the special province of a few people with natural talent. They could be developed by anyone willing to accept Huna, at least as a working hypothesis.

This, in fact, is the way Huna ought to be accepted at first. Unlike many mystical systems of thought which demand unquestioning faith without a knowledge of how they work, Huna encourages questions and growth in understanding, for it is an open-ended system without dogma and without any claim of completeness. It is not necessary to *believe* in Huna, only to be willing to try it. Just as a scientist composes a hypothesis, that is, a supposition tentatively accepted to provide a basis for his experiments before he carries them out, so the student of Huna must tentatively accept its principles as fact before attempting to make them work. If a hypothesis proves to be untrue and the results are not those expected, then the hypothesis can be rejected. But if the expected results are attained, then faith is replaced by confidence. Just as in any scientific experiment, however, if the first principles are not followed to the letter, then the onus of failure must be laid on the experimenter and not on the hypothesis.

## WORLD TRACES

Carrying his researches farther, Long began to inspect the religious literature of the world for possible traces of Huna, concentrating on those works in which secret teachings were implied. This he accomplished by translating passages back into Hawaiian, examining the root meanings of the words thus translated, and translating the results back into English. In this way he made some truly astounding discoveries, particularly in regard to the New Testament. Either Jesus himself or the earliest Christian writers were obviously initiates of Huna or somehow had an intimate knowledge of the teachings that form its basis. Time after time the principles of Huna were shown to have been hidden right within the outer teachings themselves.

Now it is extremely important to recognize that Long was not providing a reinterpretation of the Bible on the basis of a personal revelation. Nor was he applying an arbitrary system of hidden meanings to the Scriptures. What he did can be duplicated by anyone with a good Hawaiian dictionary and a knowledge of Huna symbology. Anyone who has doubts can repeat the process for himself. See the Appendix for a fuller discussion of the code language.

Further clear traces of Huna, or at least of some esoteric teaching virtually identical with it, have been found in Egyptian, Chinese, and Indian writings, but research in this area is still in its infancy. Quite recently, definite indications have been found that the secret language of Huna was used in certain Greek place names, and this opens up many exciting possibilities for further investigation.

Equally as important as the code language traces are the traces of Huna ideas and concepts that have been found all over the world. These findings have been so extensive that one cannot help at first wondering whether it is simply a matter of calling everything Huna. But two vital facts argue against this. First of all, the Huna system was found in isolation from other civilizations, logical, consistent and comprehensive. Second, other systems, compared to Huna, are fragmentary; they contain only a part of what Huna teaches, and frequently in garbled form. While studying Huna, one is constantly amazed at how it ties together previously met ideas and gives them a sense and consistency they never had before.

## An Open System

Huna is not exclusive. There is no call to abandon all other beliefs, creeds, and modes of thought before accepting Huna. A person can be a Huna Buddhist, Catholic, Protestant, scientist, psychologist, or what have you, as long as he or she recognizes Huna in his own system and uses it. Or a person can use only Huna, pure and simple. Huna is nonexclusive in another sense as well. It recognizes that there are many paths available to reach a given goal, whether spiritual, mental, or physical. Apart from its basic working hypothesis and its moral code, Huna is concerned only with *effectiveness.* The techniques used for reaching goals in other systems are perfectly valid for use in Huna as long as they work.

And, as mentioned previously, Huna does not claim

8

to be complete. There is unlimited room for expansion of ideas, concepts, techniques, knowledge, and practice. In an infinite, multidimensional universe, only a closed system with limited knowledge and rigid dogma would even dare to claim that it contained all knowledge. The basic principles of Huna have been discovered through direct experience by thousands of people, but the ways in which those principles can manifest are truly without limit.

### THE BASIC PRINCIPLES

The most fundamental idea in Huna philosophy is that we each create our own personal experience of reality, by our beliefs, interpretations, actions and reactions, thoughts and feelings. It is not that our reality is created for us as a result of these personal expressions, but that we are creators, cocreators with the Universe itself. Huna is all about learning to do that consciously. This idea, however, is not unique to Huna. It is shared, though often only in the esoteric teachings by virtually every religion known to man. Sadly, it is seldom widely taught or practiced.

Our modern tendency to separate religion from other aspects of life is an arbitrary and false form of classification. The Huna notion is that all systems, categories and classifications are our own inventions, and that it would be entirely possible to reclassify everything in a different way. It isn't that making classifications is wrong in itself as long as it serves a useful purpose, but the Huna position is that it's important to remember that we are the classifiers and behind all systems is that essential unity.

That essential unity is what we call God, which, as it happens, doesn't mean the same thing to everyone. In Huna, God and the Universe (meaning everything that is, was or will be) are one and the same. All the founders of all the world's great religions agree with that, though their followers tend to get hung up on classifications and separations. The name for this eternal, infinite presence in Hawaiian is *Kumulipo*, usually translated as "source of life," but which can also mean "the great Mystery." More important, each of the syllables of that name carries a connotation of "union," signifying that union with that mystery is both possible and desirable. And it is no accident that both syllables of *Huna*, "the secret," also carry meanings of union.

While different Huna teachers may present the principles in various ways, the following summary describes the principles as taught and practiced by the Order of Huna International:

1. *The World Is What You Think It Is.* This is the cornerstone principle of Huna, and it means that you create your own personal experience of reality through your beliefs, expectations, attitudes, desires, fears, judgements, feelings, and consistent or persistent thoughts and actions. This principle also contains the idea that by changing your thinking you can change your world.

2. *There Are No Limits.* There are no real boundaries between you and your body, you and other people, you and the world, or you and God. Any divisions used for discussion are terms of function and convenience. In other words, separation is only a useful illusion. An additional meaning of this principle is that there are unlimited potentials for creativity. You can create, in some form or another, anything you can conceive.

3. *Energy Flows Where Attention Goes.* The thoughts and feelings that you dwell on, in full awareness or not, form the blueprint for bringing into your life the nearest available equivalent experience to those same thoughts and feelings. Directed attention is the channel for the flow of biological as well as cosmic energy.

4. *Now Is the Moment of Power.* You are not bound by any experience of the past, nor by any perception of the future. You have the power in the present moment to

change limiting beliefs and consciously plant the seeds for a future of your choosing. As you change your mind you change your experience, and there is no real power outside of you, for God is within. You are free to the degree that you realize this and act upon it.

5. *To Love Is To Be Happy With.* The universe exists because of love, in its two aspects of being and becoming. Human beings exist because of love, even when they don't acknowledge it. When they do acknowledge love, they are happy as they are *and* happy in becoming more. In Huna, love involves the creation of happiness. It is not just a side effect. Everything works better, is better, when this principle is followed consciously. For very practical reasons, then, love is the only ethic needed in Huna.

6. *All Power Comes From Within.* As mentioned above, there is no power outside of you because the power of God, or the Universe, works through you in your life. You are the active channel for that power; your choices and decisions direct it. No other person can have power over you or your destiny unless you decide to let him or her have it.

7. *Effectiveness Is The Measure Of Truth.* In an infinite universe, which Huna postulates, there cannot be an absolute truth. Instead, there must be an effective truth at an individual level of consciousness. This principle is an utterly practical one which allows you to organize and act upon information in the most suitable way for the purpose at hand, so that "facts" do not get in the way of effectiveness. Any organization or system of knowledge is seen as convenient, not factual, because a different organization of the same knowledge could be just as valid for other purposes. Another way of saying this is that all systems are arbitrary, so feel free to use what works.

All the techniques used in Huna stem from applications of these principles. What makes Huna so useful for self-development is that it is based on principles, not techniques, and so we always seek out the simplest techniques that will serve the purpose. Once you know the principles you can understand the true nature of all techniques and create your own.

Now your self development is in your hands, and this book is a tool for developing your self. As you use it and live with its ideas, keep in mind the essence of the Huna philosophy, these deceptively simple guidelines for the practice of Huna:

*Bless the Present.*
*Trust yourself.*
*Expect the best.*

As the power behind these simple statements is understood and experienced, you become more and more able to create your own happiness and to direct your own destiny.

## WHY NOW?

The question may also be asked: Why are kahunas spreading the secrets of Huna now? It has been fashionable in recent years to answer such a question by saying that a "veil" is lifting from the mind of man and he is now able to grasp the truths because of some spiritual dispensation, or that the "New Age" is upon us and man has finally evolved to the proper receptive state.

The facts are much simpler than that. The danger of persecution for alternate views is slight today, at least in the United States. In today's world science and technology have not brought the happiness they promised. Organized religion is breaking down and people are searching for more meaningful and direct relationships with God. "New Thought" teachings have been around for quite a number of years and broken new ground. The human potential movement has opened many people to areas of perception they never knew existed. This list could go on for quite a while. The facts are many, but still simple. A steady and pervasive cultural change is taking place, an opening to a fuller understanding of our hidden potentials.

So here is Huna—as old as the oldest truths known to man, as new as the most modern theories of quantum physics. You can add Huna to the best of what you already know, or add what you know to Huna. Either way, it's time for people to know what they are truly capable of.

# 1

## Your Three Selves

We are each unique. Each of us experiences life a
little differently, and no two of us express quite the same
combination of talents and skills. Yet, for all the differences, we all share the same basic urge toward mastery
of ourselves and of the world around us. The urge is
called by many names and clothed in many forms, but it
is present in every human being. Dominant in the
world today is the philosophy of achieving mastery of life
by forceful control—of emotions, of people, of situations,
and of the environment. Obviously, this approach
doesn't work very well. Now here is a practical alternative, a philosophy that says we create our own reality, that
we have the power to change it, and that the way to
start is by mastering—in a loving way—our hidden self.

According to the philosophy of Huna, each of us has
three selves: a subconscious self, a conscious self,
and a superconscious self. All three are aspects of a
whole, yet they have separate functions and must inter-
act as a team in order for a person to have a healthy,

14

happy, fulfilling life. When for some reason there is disorder or conflict between them, the result can be physical or mental illness and disrupted social or environmental conditions.

Most modern psychologies accept the idea of a conscious and subconscious mind, though few have yet gotten as far as the superconscious. As for the Huna concept, the superconscious is not God in the sense of a Supreme Being. It is more like God Within, the Christ Self, or the Buddha Nature of the individual. Another way to think of it is as a sort of guardian angel. The ancient kahunas did believe in an Ultimate Being—Kumulipo—which would equate nicely with the highest Western concepts of God. But, having an eminently practical attitude toward life, they felt that this Being was so far beyond ordinary experience that it was a waste of time to speculate on its nature.

Besides the three forms of consciousness and, of course, a physical body, each person has two other components: an *aka* body, and *mana*. *Aka* is a Hawaiian term that is somewhat equivalent to *astral* or *ether* in English. *Plasma* could be another English equivalent. It is the stuff of which the physical universe is made; another term is "universal substance." An *aka* body is a quasiphysical field that surrounds and interpenetrates the physical body, and I will have more to say about it later. *Mana* is the force or energy behind life, thought, and practices termed magical for lack of understanding.

### AN ANALOGY

Let me try to bring this rather abstract explanation down to a concrete level through the use of analogy, remembering that analogies are never perfect.

You have probably seen and heard the televised account of the astronauts walking on the moon. Try to recall in your mind an image of one of those spacesuited men. Relating to Huna, now, the space suit could be likened to the physical body. From the outside it seems to have a life of its own, but all activity and purpose leave it when the man inside takes it off and hangs it up. In effect, it is dead, lifeless, without the inner man. The physical body of the astronaut, in this context, can be likened to the subconscious mind. It moves the arms and legs of the suit/body in a more or less automatic way. The mind of the astronaut plays the same role here as does the conscious mind in Huna, i.e., it gives direction and purpose to the entire physical being.

*Aka* is something like the air inside and outside the suit (you may remember the bright glow around the astronauts that looked like an aura), and the powerpack on the back of the suit supplies the energy (*mana*) that both operates the suit and provides life for the two inner selves. The powerpack also furnishes the energy to maintain contact with Houston (the superconsciousness). Houston, like the superconscious, gives encouragement and advice and knowledge, but never help unless it is asked for or unless there is danger that the mission will not be carried out.

### THE SEVEN ELEMENTS OF THE INDIVIDUAL

Although the kahuna has many ways of describing the individual, I am using one here that lists seven elements, six of which have already been mentioned:

1. *The Subconscious.* This is frequently called "the Low Self" by those who have studied the works of Max Freedom Long, but this is not meant to be derogatory. In Huna, the proper term would be *ku*, or sometimes *unihipili.*

2. *The Conscious Mind.* "Middle Self" is another term used by Long, but like "Low Self" it can be misleading. This is *lono* or *uhane* in Huna.

3. *The Superconscious.* "High Self" was the designation given by Long, and it is good in certain ways. But calling the three selves low, middle, and high causes many problems in understanding because these terms

have so many different connotations. Even the common association of the subconscious with the body, the conscious with the brain, and the superconscious with some kind of spiritual essence floating way above your head really isn't justified either physiologically or in Huna philosophy. The superconscious is *aumakua* in Huna, and also *kumupa'a* or *'ao'ao*.

4. *The Soul.* For the sake of simplicity and practicality the soul is not often discussed because it doesn't have a function and it can't be trained. It simply exists. It is the essence of your being, your personal identity, your awareness of being aware. The Huna term is *iho*.

5. The *aka* body of the individual.

6. The *mana* of the individual.

7. The physical body, or *kino*.

THE SUBCONSCIOUS

The roots of the word *ku* give us an interesting picture of the subconscious or Low Self from the kahuna point of view. The roots reveal among other things a self that can set up or establish things (like habits), that can change into something else or move from one state of experience into another, that likes to feel in control of situations, that may act spontaneously without regard for others, that can have positive or negative complexes, and that seeks peace, freedom, and relaxation. The root meanings of *unihipili* are very similar and include the ideas of acting as a servant, acting secretly or in a hidden way, and of becoming very attached to people, places, and certain ways of doing things. We have here from the Hawaiian language an excellent image of the subconscious that conforms very well to the understanding of modern Western psychology. It is discussed more fully in chapters 2 and 3.

The subconscious reasons like a computer, drawing conclusions from a given premise or experience. Contrary to some popular thinking, the subconscious is never illogical, irrational, or unreasonable. Everything it does is according to strict logic, but often we are not conscious of the premises that it uses to draw conclusions and undertake action. Also, the subconscious reasons both deductively (which means it can take a general principle or belief and apply it to specific situations) and inductively (which means it can take a specific experience and derive from it a general principle or belief). An example of the former might be a belief learned in childhood from one's parents that sex is bad. Unless the belief were changed, the subconscious would act accordingly in every specific sexual situation for the rest of one's life. An example might be a woman who had a bad experience with the first man in her life, and her subconscious acts as if all men are rotten from then on.

Memory is a function of the subconscious, in fact its only function, since all of its other functions derive from memory. When we consciously decide to remember something, we are actually eliciting the cooperation of our subconscious. If for some reason it doesn't cooperate, then we have that common experience of being unable to recall something that we are sure we know.

The subconscious is constantly communicating with the conscious mind, but our society has not put a high priority on this type of communication, so most people can't take advantage of this valuable resource. It "speaks" through dreams, imagination, feelings, physical sensations, and slips of the tongue.

### The Conscious Self

The Hawaiian word for the conscious or Middle Self, *lono*, contains meanings of awareness, communication, desire, thought, and achievement. *Uhane* also contains the idea of giving life and spirit, or direction and purpose. One of the most important functions of the conscious mind is that of giving direction to the subconscious. It is amazing how many people believe that they are supposed to take orders from their subconscious. A feeling arises or a sensation occurs, and they think they *must* act on it. All that is happening, though, is that the subconscious is giving a message and waiting for direction. If no direction is forthcoming, the subconscious will act out of habit or according to someone else's direction. The conscious mind was intended to be the master, but seldom is. An important part of Huna practice is to regain this natural order.

The conscious self communicates through speech, writing or drawing, physical action, dramatization, and thought. It has the same reasoning capability as the subconscious, but it can also "jump" reason by creative insight. Probably the greatest talent of the conscious self is that of being able to imagine what isn't. The subconscious can only imagine what has been and create new combinations out of old experience, but the conscious self can create completely new ideas and experience.

### THE SUPERCONSCIOUS

The superconscious or High Self is a dual entity, both male and female in a special way. The word *aumakua* carries the idea of a "parental spirit" and a "guardian." The *aumakua* can also be called the "Source Self," since it is the source of individual life, purpose and expression. In that respect it is the God Within, and the kahunas treat it as an inner being rather than as a spirit that lives in the sky someplace. For the individual it gives guidance, information, and inspiration, but does not give orders. It is sad to see someone waiting for his Higher Self to tell him what to do, because it just won't happen. Once the person decides for himself what to do, however, the superconscious makes available an abundance of ideas, knowledge, and energy to carry it out. Huna offers many ways of enhancing this inspirational contact.

The superconscious communicates through the channels used by the other two selves, as well as through

19

direct inspiration. When this happens, you suddenly know something, and the knowing is accompanied by a deep sense of peace, or a peaceful kind of excitement.

## THE SOUL

The most useful thing to be said about the soul is that it can expand, contract, change location in space or time, and even be multidimensional. *Iho* and its roots mean core, heart, center, self, something more, to leave and/or return, to enter, to intermarry, joy and happiness, to grow vigorously.

In English we often use the Latin word *ego* to mean the self (in Latin it means I), but the concept has become very distorted because of a mixture of other meanings from different sources. Freud used the term in psychoanalysis to mean the part of the mind that resolves conflicts between a storehouse of impulses he called the *id*, the environment, and a kind of conscience he called the *superego*. In addition, many religions and philosophies which hold that there is something inherently sinful or bad about humans have used the same term to mean self *as opposed* to others. Often they advocate diminishing or even destroying the ego, and as a result many people end up hating themselves and all their natural desires and urges.

When people ask me what Huna teaches about the ego, I first have to find their frame of reference. If it is Freudian, I just say we don't even use the concept. Freud made up a system that was useful in many ways, but it doesn't have anything to do with Huna. If the reference is to the self, I say that far from seeking to diminish it, we seek to expand it as much as possible because the more we experience the Universe as our self, the more harmony and love we can create in it. Conflict always comes from a belief in separation. Let us diminish the separation, not the self.

## THE AKA BODY

When trying to relate Huna to Western science and

psychology, we have the most trouble with the aka body because orthodox science and psychology don't accept it as real yet. For a correlation we have to turn to "psychic" science or parapsychology and the theory of ectoplasm, also called bioplasm by the Russians and psi plasma by some American parapsychologists. Astral and/or etheric bodies are other metaphysical terms for the same thing.

The *aka* body is close to the physical, but more tenuous than air, so that it completely penetrates the physical body and surrounds it like an atmosphere or aura. To those who can see it well, this body is more or less bright and glittering, changing shape and color with every thought and emotion. The *aka* body holds the pattern for every cell and organ in the body, so that growth, repair, and maintenance can proceed smoothly. The *aka* body is very sensitive to thought, however, so that distorted thoughts held for any length of time may distort the pattern and eventually the physical body as well.

One Huna working theory has it that everything that we come into contact with through any of our senses is forever linked to us by an *aka* "thread" between the object and our *aka* body. Another working theory from Huna that might be considered more "modern" is one that suggests a universal field of *aka* in which individuals, locations, and objects are differentiated only by their unique frequency vibration. By "attuning" your mind to the right frequency, you can make contact with anything in the universe, and your subconscious retains the frequency memory of anything you come into contact with through your senses. Neither of these two theories is more true than the other in Huna terms, for truth is what works for the individual.

## MANA

*Mana* has three basic meanings in kahuna teaching, which sometimes causes confusion among students. The most fundamental meaning is "power," whether divine or not. The other two basic meanings deriving from that are "authority/confidence" and "energy."

"Power" means "to be able," and this applies equally to skills, attitudes, and energy that can do work. In the history books it is recorded that King Kamehameha, who united the Hawaiian Islands, had a great deal of *mana*. Now some have taken this to mean that he had an abundance of divine energy flowing through him, but it is more likely that those who said it were referring to the fact of his absolute authority as ruler, or even to the unshakable confidence that enabled him to achieve his goals.

*Mana* is not just ability, just confidence, or just energy, but actually refers to all three working together. The kahunas had words to use for confidence (*paulele, hilina'i*), authority (*kuleana, hano*), skills (*loea, akamai*) and energy, (*mahi, uila*) when they wanted to make distinctions. They used *mana* when they meant the combination. A kahuna uses *mana* in the process of healing, which means he uses mentally directed energy, confidence, authority, and skill. This is his "power." In the same way, everyone has *mana* to some degree or another, which can be increased or diminished according to circumstances.

Nevertheless, in introductory teachings *mana* is usually equated with terms like *ch'i, prana, orgone, od,* and others which refer to life energy, bioenergy and even emotional energy, although the more correct Huna term for these would be *ki*, the same word sound as used in Japanese. By learning to increase and direct *mana* as energy, you also increase your skill, your confidence, your authority, your power in general.

### THE PHYSICAL BODY

*Kino*, the physical body, has roots, which mean "a highly energized thought form." In Huna teaching your body is a materialized thought of your High Self, modified by the acquired attitudes and habits of your conscious and subconscious minds. Because of this, the condition of your body—its appearance and state of health—can to a very large extent be altered by changing your attitudes and habits, in other words your self-image and your behavior. Your body responds instantly on a cellular level to your every thought and feeling. Most often this takes the form of muscular or organic tension or release. By learning to master (i.e., direct) your thoughts and feelings, you can thus exert tremendous influence on your body. If you attempt to control or repress your thoughts and feelings, however, your body will rebel, instantly or eventually, with pain and/or disfunction.

Your physical body is *kino*, but so is your physical world. That is, your personal world, your particular environment as you experience it, is not only perceived by you... it is formed by you, especially by your thoughts, feelings, beliefs, expectations, fears and judgments about it. One of the most significant "secret facts about you" taught in Huna is your ability to form—and reform—your personal world experience.

# 2

# Huna and Modern Psychology

Huna psychology differs in many ways from the Western forms of psychology with which most Americans are familiar. But far more important than the differences are the similarities, because these show an underlying unity of direct experience. Comparing Huna and the ideas of several Western proponents of psychological theory will throw some light on the hidden self and how it can be mastered.

## HUNA AND FREUD

The most famous Western psychological theorist is undoubtedly Sigmund Freud. Like the kahunas, he divided the human mind into three parts, which he called the *id*, the *ego*, and the *superego*. Although the meanings of the terms are not equivalent, the kahuna's three-part division corresponds in some ways to Freud's.

*Id* was Freud's name for what he considered an animalistic, primitive, passion-ruled, and impulse-driven part of the mind that was also a reservoir of

24

unresolved and deeply hidden conflicts. It had to be controlled or else it would become wildly destructive. The kahuna's concept of a *ku* connotes a hidden part of the mind that could also be a reservoir for unresolved conflicts. It is animalistic in the sense that it is directly linked to the functioning of the body, and it serves to channel instincts and emotions. But in the kahuna view *ku* does not have to be controlled, only taught or trained. The *ku* is the reservoir not only of unresolved conflicts, but of all learning and habits, and its instinctive drives have to do with survival, growth, and happiness. All the negative effects produced by the *ku* are considered as the result of learned behavior and beliefs, whereas the negative effects produced by the *id* are thought of as due to its very nature. Basically, Freud and the kahunas agree that there is a hidden part of the mind that affects much of our behavior and experience, but Freud thought it was inherently bad and the kahunas think it is inherently good. For the sake of convenience in discussion, we will call that part of the mind the "subconscious," though neither Freud nor the kahunas would be completely happy with the term.

Freud and the kahunas are in agreement about placing our various complexes in the subconscious. For both the negative complex is a tangled mass of unrationalized thought patterns which can cause neurotic behavior and/or physical illness. These complexes can be caused by traumatic incidents or by the construction of associations in early life. Sometimes we are not in a mental or emotional condition to rationalize (make logical and acceptable) a trauma when it occurs or an association when it is made. Then the thought patterns instituted at that time might cause intense guilt at a later date when we are confronted with a situation which contradicts the subconscious thought pattern. In Huna and Freudian psychology, it is understood that the complex may remain completely hidden from the conscious mind until brought to light through special analytical techniques. However, for Freud these techniques are essential, and for the kahunas they are merely useful.

The analytical techniques used by Freudians and by the kahunas are amazingly similar. Dreams, memories, and childhood experiences are all utilized as means of discovering the content of the complex. For the Freudians, once the complex is found it is supposed to dissipate by the simple fact of being made conscious. One of the main problems of such psychoanalysis is that the dissipation doesn't always take place. Often a more active phase of undoing and remaking the complex is required, and at this the kahunas excel. Like Freud, the kahunas recognize that guilt feelings are the activating principle behind most negative complexes. Unlike Freud, they realize that guilt feelings are not all sexually based. Furthermore, they understand the extremely important role of penance and forgiveness in breaking up and dissolving a complex. The subconscious is very impressed by any kind of physical stimulus. Fasting, purification rites, and the giving of a share of one's possessions to those in need play a large part in the psychotherapy of the kahunas.

The problem of guilt is treated very practically by the kahunas. In Western society the influence of Christianity, as interpreted by most of that religion's leaders, has promoted the idea that one can sin against God as well as against man. To the kahunas, sinning against God is as inconceivable as an atom sinning against man. It can't be done even if you want to. The only type of sin they recognize is intentional hurt to another being, either physical, mental, or emotional. Thus the only one who can forgive sin is the being that was hurt. In all cases the kahunas will first have the person seek forgiveness from the injured one. If this is impractical for some reason, they then resort to some other means of expiating the guilt in a way that is convincing to the subconscious. This type of self-forgiveness is also

used in cases of guilt where there has been no hurt
to another, which is a common Western problem.

Freud considered the ego to be the conscious, reasoning part of the mind. It was pictured as constantly
struggling against the wild and unruly desires of the id
and trying to reconcile them with the demands of
the superego. The innate cooperation of conscious and
subconscious was not recognized by Freud, partly
because he almost totally separated mind and body. The
kahunas, teaching that the subconscious controls most
of the bodily functions and some of the mental, believe
that the subconscious has to be treated somewhat
like a child by the conscious self and trained to cooperate
in the development of the whole person. This, in fact,
is one of the reasons for the existence of the conscious
mind: it has to act as teacher or guide for the subconscious. Naturally, the first step is to realize the
existence of the subconscious as a portion of the mind
with a particular function.

Freud's superego has no relation to the High Self
(*aumakua*) of Huna. In simple terms the superego stands
for conscience, that which tells us whether we are doing
right or wrong. In the Huna system this function is
divided between the conscious and the subconscious.
The conscious mind (*lono*) can tell right from wrong
through a process of reasoning, but the subconscious
(*ku*) must rely on learned habits, whether the *lono* played
an active part in that learning or not. Thus, if a child
is repeatedly taught that dancing is a sin, his subconscious will keep that idea as a memory of truth
because the conscious *lono* was unable to reason otherwise at the time. In adult life the act of dancing will
always be considered as something wrong and sinful
until and unless the conscious is able to look at the
memory of the early teaching and rationalize it in the
light of more recently acquired knowledge. In this
respect the *ku* acts as a sort of unconscious conscience.

The concept of the libido, so controversial among

Freudians and non-Freudians alike, has a direct application to Huna. For Freud it was psychic energy, but without the occult connotations which that term has now. It was supposed to arise out of the sexual desires and be the motive force behind the positive, loving instincts of humanity. If misdirected or blocked from its proper functioning, the force degenerates into lust, or else becomes static and binds together the elements of the negative complex. It is not clear whether Freud ever meant the libido to be more than a working concept, but the equivalent Huna concept of *mana* is accepted by the kahunas as being very real. Like the libido, it can be directed to positive and negative ends. However, it is thought to be blocked by the complexes rather than binding them. If the complexes are not too strong, *mana* can still flow in a restricted way.

### HUNA AND JUNG

Carl Jung developed the ideas of the persona and the anima/animus, which correspond fairly well to the *lono* and *ku*, respectively. The persona, as the outer mask of the person, is easily recognizable as the conscious *lono*. Jung's concept of the ego, considered by him to be partly conscious and partly unconscious, has that same relationship to the *lono* and *ku*. As something which is reflective of personal experience, ego resembles the *ku*; as part of the outer expression of the individual, it takes on *lono* qualities. Emotional disturbance was seen by Jung as a form of disharmony between the persona, ego, and anima or animus. (The collective unconscious was also involved in this, but let us ignore that for a moment.) The kahunas see emotional disturbance as a disharmony between the *lono* and *ku*, in which the emotional expression itself is of the *ku's* making. Jung also gave great importance to personality types. When a person becomes too extreme in expressing his type, emotional problems are to be expected. In the Huna view, this would be the equivalent of a particular complex acquiring excessive dominance over the total person.

With Jung's concept of the collective unconscious, we come closest to the Huna High Self or superconscious, though there is a strong admixture of *ku* activity. Jung was impressed by the fact uncovered in his research that emotionally disturbed people in so-called civilized societies frequently produced symbolic representations in their unconscious and semiconscious states which resembled the symbolic productions of so-called primitive peoples. This led him to the idea of a hereditary or ancestral memory, and thence to a collective human consciousness, or rather unconsciousness. Actually, this collective unconscious does not resemble the individual *aumakua* (High Self) of the kahunas so much as what they call the *po'e aumakua*, or Great Company of High Selves. Every High Self is supposed to be in contact with every other High Self, and for certain purposes—for instance when specifically requested—they can work in concert. This active idea goes somewhat beyond Jung's concept, but the similarity is close enough to be significant. The Great Company could naturally be the source of a common symbology, as well as inspiration and guidance for the individual. As a source of memory for ancestral experience, the kahunas might accept Jung's concept in part, but there is also the factor of *ku* memory to consider. The *ku* contains not only the memory of this life but of all previous lives, for kahunas believe in reincarnation, so a certain amount of ancestral memory could also be personal memory.

Jung's view of the libido was closer to the Huna idea of *mana* than was Freud's. Jung differed from Freud in that he saw the libido or life force as neutral in character rather than specifically genital. For the kahunas, too, it is neutral, ready to be employed for good or evil, and related to the whole person. However, Jung never reached the stage of considering it as a real, tangible force that can be consciously manipulated.

## HUNA AND REICH

It is in the work of Wilhelm Reich that we encounter a force which approaches the Huna concept of *mana* so closely as to be almost uncanny. Unfortunately, few people have yet heard of the work of this brilliant scientist and philosopher. Reich was a former disciple of Freud, but like Jung and others, he was forced to make a break for reasons of principle. Among other things, Reich developed a theory and structure of character analysis which is used by many psychoanalysts today. This was intimately tied with Freud's own concept of the libido, which Reich carried to its logical conclusion.

Far from using the libido as a mere convenience, Reich grew to believe that it was an actual form of energy which not only kept the body alive, but which played a direct role in the formation of complexes. While studying character traits, Reich discovered a series of muscle groupings which remained chronically tensed in the neurotic person. When these muscles were released through various manipulative techniques, the person would experience a cathartic emotional release that was intimately tied to the existing complexes. What is more, such persons also reported a sensation of "currents" or "streamings" which flowed through the body. In Huna a healthy person is expected to be able to feel the flow of *mana* in the body. This flow is not only necessary for good physical and mental health; it is vitally necessary in order to contact the High Self at will and partake of its greater energy. To feel the flow means that the *ku* is relatively free of restrictive complexes. Reich discovered the physical basis for this phenomenon and came to virtually the same conclusions independently.

One of the characteristics of *mana* is that it can be willed out of the body and into an object, charging it, so to speak. In former times the kahunas were said to charge throwing sticks with their *mana*. During a battle they would throw the sticks over the heads of their own warriors, and whenever the sticks would hit an enemy, no matter how slightly, the discharge of *mana* would knock him unconscious. There are reports of Indian medicine men and practitioners of the martial arts who can knock a man down with the touch of a finger, and those who are familiar with the work of Mesmer may recall that he did the same thing.

Reich performed an experiment which demonstrated this effect, though much less violently. He took a rubber glove and brought it near an electroscope, a device which measures positive and negative charges, to show that there was no reaction. Then he placed the glove over the solar plexus of a healthy subject for a few minutes. When he again brought the glove near the electroscope, there was a very definite reaction. Something had obviously been transferred from the person to the glove. Further experiments by Reich proved that it was not any known form of electromagnetism. He called it "orgone energy." It is extremely interesting to note that the kahunas considered the solar plexus to be a center of bioenergy for generation and storage of *mana*.

### HUNA AND BERNE

Eric Berne developed a form of psychotherapy that he called Transactional Analysis. TA, as it is often called now, postulates a fundamental unit of social inter-course called a "transaction," which is actually no more than the stimulus and response that takes place between two people who are interacting. The nature of this transaction defines the quality of interpersonal (and probably intrapersonal) relationships, and therefore the individual's state of happiness and effectiveness. In TA there are three states that a person can shift into which determine the nature of transactions: the Parent, predominantly the subconscious recordings of the transactions between a child's two parents; the Child, the recordings of the child's feelings and responses to what he sees and hears; and the Adult, the record-ings of direct experience and resulting conclusions. In the course of relating with others, people use one of several "life positions" usually decided upon early in life, such as "I'm not OK—you're OK," and they relate to others from that position within one of the states of Parent, Child, or Adult. An important thesis of TA is that the life positions were based on decisions, and that with increased awareness and training a person can change life position to "I'm OK—you're OK" and act more and more from an Adult state of mind.

Of course, the idea that the subconscious records everything and that these recordings affect and even determine behavior is the same in Huna, as is the idea that decisions made at any age can be unmade and re-placed by new and more effective decisions. Parent, Child, and Adult are equivalent to complexes, and the kahunas would no doubt admire Berne's clever but arbitrary division of behavior patterns, even while ad-mitting the arbitrariness of their own, for all systems are no more than convenient ways of describing reality. What the kahunas would agree to most wholeheartedly is the TA direction toward an "I'm OK—you're OK" Adult state of mind and behavior.

#### HUNA AND PERLS

Frederick Perls was the founder of Gestalt therapy, the purpose of which is to promote the growth process and develop the human potential, which is also the purpose of Huna. Briefly, some of the main elements of Gestalt therapy have to do with awareness of the whole being of a person (not just his mind or just his body or just his brain); with giving feedback to the person of what his whole being is saying; with staying in the here and now; and with making no judgments or in-terpretations. All of these fit perfectly with Huna philosophy. There are many ingenious techniques used in Gestalt therapy, but Perls himself emphasized that

Gestalt is not the techniques used, that to confuse
the therapy with the techniques would be a vast error.
The therapeutic practices used in Gestalt are to integrate
attention and awareness, and any technique that does
this is valid. So in Huna, the therapeutic and developmental methods are to increase awareness; skills,
and happiness, and any techniques from any system that
aid this, including any made up on the spot, are valid.
Another similarity with Huna is Perls's readiness to
change theories as necessary and desirable. This is
equivalent to the Huna concept, "If it's useful, it's true."

## CONCLUSION

This discussion has hardly done justice to the Western
psychologies presented, much less to Huna. But at
least it shows that there is much in common between
them.

In the middle of the Pacific Ocean, out of touch with
other civilizations for hundreds of years, a group of
people was found with a psychological system as advanced as any existing today. It is well to remember that
when Western missionaries first went to Hawaii, the concept of the subconscious had not even been formulated
in the West. The Western science of psychology is
still very young. It is still playing with the mind alone,
although here and there attempts are being made to integrate it with the body. As for the spiritual part of man,
the great majority of psychologists will not even acknowledge it. In Huna we find spirit, mind, and body all
linked in one coherent system. Since it has had thousands
of years to develop, this system would seem to merit
serious study.

33

# 3

## What Your Subconscious Is Really Like

In Huna, the *ku*, or *unihipili*, is said to be "roughly" equivalent to the subconscious mind. Why "roughly"? Because there is no general agreement in the field of psychology as to exactly what the subconscious mind is. Even the most traditional psychologists cannot agree among themselves. Some consider it a reality; others conceive of it as a mental construct, a convenient reference with no basis in reality. The followers of still other psychological schools consider the "subconscious" as the seat of all the higher powers of man, confusing it in a way with what most people think of as God.

With Huna there is no such problem. The *ku* is one aspect of one's total mind which has very specific functions. For the sake of convenience, we often use the English term *subconscious* to describe it, but in many ways it is more conscious than the conscious mind of many people. Also, for the sake of convenience, we often speak of it and deal with it as a separate entity, even to the point of giving it a name of its own. However, it must be understood that the *ku* is separate only in function, not in fact. Nevertheless, because so few people are aware of how their minds work, the *ku* may sometimes seem like a total stranger, if not an enemy.

## THE NATURE OF THE SUBCONSCIOUS

The nature of the *ku* is revealed in the secret meanings of the code words that make up this name and its alternates in Hawaiian. From the code or root meanings, we find that this aspect of mind has the following functions and attributes:

1. Its primary function is memory.

2. It controls the entire operation of the physical body, though some of this control is shared by the conscious mind (*lono*).

3. It is the source of all emotions and feelings.

4. It is the source of all mental and physical habits and behavior.

5. It is the means by which the conscious mind perceives experience and acts upon it.

6. It is the receiver and transmitter of all psychic phenomena.

7. Its prime directive is to grow.

8. It reasons logically.

9. It obeys orders.

Now let us examine these functions and attributes, some of which may not seem to apply to your own subconscious at first glance.

## MEMORY

It is because of the memory function of the *ku* that we are able to learn something so well that we don't have to think about it any more except, possibly, in an emergency. Examples of this are speaking, walking, riding a bike, or driving a car. In all of these a more or less automatic process of remembering is taking place, a memory of learned patterns of behavior. Much of our memory is so close to the surface that we do not notice any time lag in our desire for it and its appearance, except when it refuses to appear for some inexplicable reason. Contrary to what many people still think, memory is not recorded in the physical brain. Some recent scientific research suggests that memories are duplicated at several sites in the body, and that the actual recording is at a purely energy level. This, in fact, is the Huna teaching. In ancient times the analogy used was that of thoughts and impressions held in clusters of astral (*aka*) matter, making up the energy body of the subconscious. A more modern analogy would be that of a computer, because the physical parts of the computer merely serve as a convenient framework for the actual memory, which is stored as magnetic fields. In computer terminology, informational input is stored in "bits." So many "bits" make a "byte," so many "bytes" make a "word," and so many "words" make a "word group."

To use this analogy for personal memory, suppose you met a person at a party last week. Each physical characteristic of that person might represent a "bit" of information. Grouped together as a "byte," they would represent the whole physical appearance of the person. What that person said and how he reacted to you might form another byte. The total impression of the person would form a "word." The entire party would be stored in your memory as a series of word groups. The outstanding impression of the evening, that which retained most of your conscious attention, would remain "on call" for a considerable period, perhaps the rest of your life if it were impressive enough. The less important impressions would remain on "available" status, while those you didn't notice at all would be placed in the general file. When you want to recall the events of the evening, your subconscious will pull out the "on call" impression first, and the "available" items in descending order of importance, depending on how long you intend to dwell on the subject. This is because the subconscious thinks by logical association.

Two things are required in order for memories to be easily recalled. First, the original impression must receive conscious attention; and second, the impression must be tied or associated to other impressions. There is a lot of information in your biocomputer, and it is much easier for your subconscious to find a "word" than to find a "bit." This is why names are frequently difficult to recall, and also why they often pop up long after you called for them. They did not have enough conscious attention on them when they first appeared, and so they were not "on call." Their coming to mind later merely indicates that it took the *ku* a while to find them. Of course, tension or anxiety can disrupt your energy field and the memory process as well.

### THE BODY

All of the process systems of the body (nervous, circulatory, muscular, energetic, digestive, etc.) are under the direct control of the subconscious mind. Most of its knowledge of how to operate these systems comes from cellular directives, such as that in the DNA molecule, but a considerable amount is received from parental and social beliefs, as well as conscious decisions and training. Biofeedback confirms the Huna insight that through the directed attention of the conscious mind, we can influence the subconscious operation of the body to a surprising extent. However, this influence can be either positive (as when its operation is improved) or negative (as when its operation is impaired). In other words, the operation of your body is influenced very directly by the way you think and feel and by what you think, as psychosomatic medicine has shown. Of course, you can consciously decide to move your arms and legs, to breathe at a different rate, and to speak loudly or softly, but even these conscious actions must be performed with the cooperation of subconscious memory and its direct link with the muscles and organs involved. Star athletes and yoga masters can perform seeming miracles with their bodies, not because they have learned to take over conscious control of their bodies, but because they have learned conscious co-operation with their subconscious to a great degree.

### EMOTIONS

In the Huna system emotions and feelings are no more and no less than movements of bioenergy accompanied by particular thoughts and/or patterns of muscle tension which distinguish them. Emotions can be stored as potential energy in muscle tension under certain conditions, but generally they are evoked on the spot by a mental, physical, or environmental stimulus. In such a case, the stimulus causes a subconscious association with a memory that evokes one of four primary energy response patterns, or a blend of two or more. On the physical level the energy for such responses comes from adrenalin/glycogen release in the body, but it may also involve biofield channeling through the meridian system, and possibly energy exchange with the environment.

The four primary energy response patterns are *fear* (withdrawal), *anger* (attack), *joy* (expansion), and *action* (mental or physical activity). Fear or fear and anger combined can get emotional energy locked up in muscle or even cellular tension. The fear/anger combination also produces various levels of depression. All of these responses and their combinations are released because of associations stored in the subconscious memory, and they will continue to be released by the same associations until the memorized patterns are changed by conscious or superconscious intervention.

### HABITS

Like emotions, mental and physical habits are learned responses stored in subconscious memory and released by associated stimuli. The energy response pattern is that of action, mentioned previously, and it may or may not be accompanied by emotion. When you jump out of the way of sudden danger, there is no emotional reaction during the jump; there is only action energy in play. Any emotion comes afterward when the mind has time to replay the event and consider what might have been.

Most of our habits are "unconscious," meaning that our conscious mind is not paying attention to what our subconscious mind is doing. In the Huna teaching if a habit no longer serves a viable purpose from the subconscious viewpoint, it will change automatically without the need for conscious awareness. However, if the habit still serves a need of some kind even though it is consciously undesirable, then it will take conscious attention to change the habit. But attention alone won't do it. In addition, the subconscious must be given a viable alternative.

The length of time that a habit has been engaged in is unimportant. The subconscious is only interested in end results, and if a new habit will produce as good or better results than an old one, the subconscious will allow change to take place easily. If the subconscious is not convinced of that, however, it may be impossible to change an old habit. The important point here is that there is no vacuum in the subconscious. The only way to get rid of an old habit is to replace it with a new one. Even becoming a nonsmoker requires the learning of new habits of not smoking in various circumstances. Also, in the Huna teaching beliefs are considered as habits, as subject to change and replacement for greater effectiveness as any other habit.

## Perception

We have conscious perception of our world through
our senses, which number far more than the basic five.
Sight, for instance, includes the abilities to sense
color, shading, depth, perspective, patterns, shapes, and
meaningfulness (as with reading). Sound includes the
sensing of pitch, tone, overtones, harmony, noise,
and meaningfulness (as with speech). Taste, of course,
includes bitter, sweet, sour, and salty; smell has at
least ten variations listed by some authors; and touch
includes pressure, texture, temperature, and a number
of other factors.

All these senses come through the nervous system
into conscious awareness, but according to Huna it is the
*ku* which monitors them so they do not overwhelm
us. *Ku* brings certain ones to our attention at particular
times for particular reasons, diminishes certain ones
in response to beliefs held, and learns and stores
the learning of how to enhance certain senses. When we
take conscious action as a result of a perception, we
are really taking action as a result of a perception filtered
through the *ku* and whatever prejudices or skills it
may have learned. Perception can be distorted slightly,
with just a minor decrease in our effectiveness, or it
can be so far out of line that we do not even share
the same experience as those around us. On the other
hand, it can be enhanced to the point where our perception is better than average, or to the point where we
can sense what others are not even aware of. All of this
depends on the state of beliefs and learned behaviors
in the *ku*.

## Psychic Phenomena

In Huna, psychic phenomena are considered as
extensions of our normal senses and not as something
completely distinct and "supranormal." In this view
psychic phenomena go on all the time in everyone's life,
but because of prejudiced beliefs they are mostly

ignored unless they are dramatic. Sometimes they are allowed to sneak into notice as hunches, intuition, inspiration, and coincidence.

Correlating Huna as closely as possible with Western terminology:

> Telepathy is an extension of our sense of hearing and ability for speech;
> Clairvoyance is an extension of our sense of sight;
> Psychokinesis is an extension of our sense of touch and our ability to physically affect our environment;
> Divination (precognition) is an extension of our ability to estimate probabilities and make educated guesses about future events.

These senses and abilities are called "psychic" or "paranormal" only because they are not as common in our culture as they are in others. This is because the *ku*, which is in charge of all the senses and abilities, has accepted cultural beliefs that say such things are either not possible or not good. People who have psychic experiences have just never accepted those cultural beliefs, and people who have been trained in this area have simply overcome those beliefs. Since it is a matter of belief and not human nature, everyone can experience "psychic" phenomena and be trained in the proficient use of psychic abilities.

## GROWTH

The definition of growth in Huna terms is "to increase awareness, skills, and happiness." This applies to all forms of consciousness, from atoms to galaxies, whether animal, vegetable, or mineral. In humans the urge toward growth is located in the *ku*.

There are some who think that our primary urge is for survival and that only after survival is taken care of do we turn to "higher" pursuits, like art and culture. This is why popular movies and stories so often show our ancestors as practically beast-like predators or gatherers with nothing on their minds except food, sex, and killing. But the actual traces found by archeologists and anthropologists show that even the earliest humans were inventors, artists, and craftsmen, in the midst of the harshest environmental conditions. It is the urge toward growth that ensures survival, and not the other way around.

Curiosity is part of the urge toward increasing awareness. It is this urge that helps a baby develop by exploring its environment, and it is the same urge that drives adult explorers, inventors, and scientists. The urge to increase skills (both in number and quality) helps us to apply what we have learned from our expanding awareness. And the urge toward increasing happiness spurs us on toward better and better ways of doing things, mentally, physically, spiritually, and socially. In fact, the only thing that keeps any of us from becoming demigods is fear, the fear-producing beliefs that interfere with the *ku*'s natural progress toward fulfillment.

## Logic

Of all the misconceptions that people have about the subconscious, the most detrimental is that it is irrational or illogical. On the contrary, as already pointed out, the *ku* is every bit as rational and logical as a computer. That, you could say, is the problem.

People think the subconscious is irrational because it acts contrary to what they consciously want in the moment, and because it seems to act that way without any apparent reason. The key word here is *apparent*. Your *ku* is *always* acting on the basis of an assumption— a belief about reality—accepted as true at some point in your life. And the *ku* will always follow and act out that assumption to its logical conclusions, whatever they are and whatever you consciously think about them at the time.

Of course, the situation gets more complicated when there are conflicting assumptions about the same area of life. Just imagine the problems a computer would have if you fed it conflicting information. It would have to choose on its own which assumption to follow in any given situation. But its choice would be quite logical within the framework of its memory and programming (learned habits).

If you think that the *ku* is illogical, then any attempt to change it has to be haphazard and a matter of luck. But once you know it is completely logical, then all you have to do is "convince it" to follow another set of assumptions and attitudes. The fact that hypnosis works, as an example, is proof that this concept is valid.

#### OBEDIENCE

The subconscious is not an unruly, rebellious child, nor does it ever work against your best interests *from its point of view.* Whenever the *ku* seems to be opposing you, it is because it is following previous orders that you either gave it or allowed to remain. And it *has* to follow previous orders until they are replaced. If the *ku* is producing unpleasant physical symptoms, it is to avoid something worse, and because it has not been taught any viable alternatives. Just thinking of an alternative with the conscious mind isn't enough. New orders have to be given through training in new habits. Success in establishing new habits depends on how well they serve one or more of the three aspects of growth, taking into account existing beliefs of what is or isn't possible, and what is or isn't good.

The main thing to remember is that your *ku* will serve you faithfully and quickly, as soon as you learn to give good orders.

# 4

# Your Conscious Mind

Nearly everyone has a mistaken idea about the nature
of the conscious mind. René Descartes wrote, "I think,
therefore I am," but that statement has little meaning unless you define what thinking is. Is it the picturing
of images in the mind? The step-by-step process of
logic? Is it intuitive feelings? The translation of sensory
input into sense-making data? The comparison of
previous experiences to present ones? Is "thinking" all
of these, some, or none?

There are those who say that what distinguishes
the conscious mind from the subconscious is awareness.
But it is well known that the subconscious can be influenced by what other people say when the conscious
mind is totally unaware of it, as during sleep, while
in shock, or under an anesthetic. And it is also well known
that in a hypnotic or meditative state information can
be obtained from the subconscious mind about past
events of which the conscious mind was not aware at all.
So the conscious mind cannot be distinguished

by the faculty of awareness.

Others may say that only the conscious mind can reason, yet this, too, is false. As already discussed there is not a single habit, attitude, or emotion held by the subconscious which is not logically derived from some basic assumption. The subconscious can reason deductively, as when a baby takes a known fact that a mother's nipple can be used for nourishment and relaxation, and deduces that bottle nipples and pacifiers (which are *quite* different in size, shape, and texture) can be used for the same or similar purposes. The subconscious can also reason inductively, as when a baby learns, through separate experiences, the general principle that crying gets attention. So reasoning is definitely not a perogative of the conscious mind.

A third attractive idea is that the conscious mind is the center of self-awareness, one's sense of personal identity. However, this idea doesn't stand up under scrutiny any better than the others. You consciously know who you are, but so does your subconscious. That is why you turn automatically at the sound of your name, why you can instantly recognize your own handwriting, and even why you can forget who you are during amnesia. That would not be possible unless the center of your identity were in the memory of your subconscious.

Let's turn, then, to the Huna view of what really makes the conscious mind unique.

## WILL POWER

Huna teaches that the primary attribute of the conscious mind is will power. Unfortunately, the concept of *will* has bothered people for ages. A man is said to have strong "will power" when, in the face of great odds, he maintains a certain course of action, or nonaction, as the case may be. Certain people are said to exert their will over others, making their victims accomplish things against their will. There are people who are said to be able to "will" things to happen, and people with weak wills are supposed to be easily manipulated by those with stronger wills.

If you are to understand the conscious mind, you must understand the nature of will power. Much of the misunderstanding of what the will really is has been brought about by the use of the word *power* in conjunction with it. Power can be defined in one sense as a faculty or ability. The problem is that this definition doesn't explain anything. We can speak of the power of sight and understand that it means the ability to see. We can speak of the power of an optic lens and know that it means the lens has the ability to magnify an object so many times. But to speak of the power of will as the ability to will, or even the faculty of willing, leaves us just as confused as ever until we define will itself.

According to Webster's *New World Dictionary*, the word *will* has several meanings. One is "the power of making a reasoned choice or decision." This is most definitely an attribute of the conscious mind. In fact, Huna teaches that it is the primary attribute of the conscious mind, usually describing it as "the ability to direct awareness and attention." It may be interesting to note that the Hawaiian word for "choice or decision" is *holo*, which has a root meaning of "to put forth effort for achievement" and which uses a root of the word *lono*, the conscious mind. *Lono*, by the way, also has a root meaning of "to achieve (*lo*) desires (*ono*)."

The only real ability you have consciously is that of directing your awareness and attention in response to thought or experience. The actual directing is called making a decision or a choice. This is what is meant by "free will." It is not the freedom to do anything you want whenever or however you want, nor to make anything happen when you want it to, nor to make others do what you want them to do, for obviously we don't have that, even though we can learn techniques to increase our effectiveness. We can't make someone like us by exerting our will. And we can't make ourselves or the world perfect in a flash just by "willing" it (which really means "wishing hard"). What we can do, however, is to choose or decide how we are going to respond to our experience of life, what we are going to do from this moment forward and in any future moment to change either ourselves or the circumstances. At any moment *of conscious awareness* we have that freedom to choose.

Now, why did I make that qualification? Nearly everyone has had the experience at one time or another of carrying out a habit without conscious awareness. It may have been something like reaching for and lighting a cigarette and not realizing what you've done until you are halfway through. It may have been while driving some place and having no conscious memory of the trip once you get there. It may have been an automatic emotional response at something someone said, with a feeling afterward that you couldn't help yourself. It may have been *anything* that you have done without being aware of doing it.

What happens in such a case is that the *ku*, your subconscious, takes over with a well-learned behavior pattern in response to some kind of mental, energetic, or physical stimulus, while at the same time your conscious mind focuses attention elsewhere, sometimes apparently blanking out. It may seem as if the subconscious is making a decision, but that is true only in the same sense that a computer makes decisions. In reality, both simply respond in a pre-set way to a memorized stimulus. In a completely new situation for which there is no pre-set program, the computer stops functioning. The subconscious relies on inspiration from the superconscious or direction from the conscious mind. If neither of these are forthcoming, for whatever reason, it also stops functioning by way of panic, paralysis of mind or body, fainting, coma, apathy, or autism. *These generally occur only if there is a belief that the conscious mind is powerless.*

It is necessary for effective living to realize that at any

moment of conscious awareness you have the power to choose how to think, feel, or act. Even if you have "gone on automatic" in some behavior pattern, the moment you become aware is the moment that you can make a decision and change the pattern. Giving in to or falling into an automatic behavior pattern, no matter how undesirable, does not mean that you are a failure, that you are worthless, and that there is no point in trying to take conscious charge of the situation. Those are invalid excuses for not taking the risk that you might fail again. As someone once said, real failure is not falling down; real failure is falling down and not getting up again.

As anyone who has tried to change a habit knows, just making the decision to change is not enough. Many people try this and then get discouraged when the old habit keeps coming back. Here is where another dictionary definition of "will" helps to explain what is needed: "a strong and fixed purpose; determination." Determination, an unswerving will, is actually the continuous, conscious directing of attention and awareness toward a given end for a given purpose. And this is accomplished by continuously renewing the decisions or choices made to reach the given end, in spite of apparent obstacles and difficulties. A person with such a will, that is, such an ability to keep renewing a decision, does not get discouraged by mistakes and failures. If one method used to reach his goal does not work after repeated tries, he tries another, and then another, until he finds one that does work, even if it means he has to change himself. A person with a so-called "weak will" is simply someone who uses the same conscious will power that everyone has to change his mind about continuing toward a goal. In other words, he just makes a different decision, a decision not to continue, while the first person makes a decision to continue. And there may be times when that is the wisest thing to do. So a "strong-willed person" is one who doesn't change his decisions easily, and a "weak-willed person" is one who does change his decisions easily. The point is that both are using the same power to make decisions.

Perhaps now you can see that it is total nonsense to speak of someone "exerting his will" over someone else. There is nothing to exert. You can get someone to do something by the threat of pain, the promise of pleasure, or the use of physical force, but not by making one decision or a hundred. If anyone does follow your will, it is for his own reasons, not yours, even if you back up your will with threats, promises, or force. It is not your will, your ability to choose, that makes others do things.

In this supposedly modern age many people still have the Dark Age notion that certain persons are endowed with supraphysical energy that enables them to use psychokinesis (the ability to move or influence objects at a distance without physical contact) on other people the way a puppeteer plays with marionettes. They confuse this supposed ability with "will power" because the word *power* has an extended meaning of energy. Now it is true that you can be influenced by another person's beliefs and emotions, and it is true that the more a person knows about you the easier it is for him to set off your automatic behavior patterns. It is also true that telepathy and psychokinesis exist. But no one can "make" you do anything against your free will. It is not another person's will that gets you to do things you don't want to do; it is your own fears, beliefs, hopes, likes and dislikes, and your automatic patterns. Another person's influence on you stops dead the moment you come to conscious awareness and decide not to be influenced any longer. The will of the strongest-willed person in the world has no power over you if you make that decision.

### ATTENTION AND AWARENESS

I said that Huna teaches that your primary conscious ability is to direct your attention and awareness.

49

What is the distinction between them?

Attention is the focus of awareness on some aspect of your mental or physical experience. It is the noticing of something more than other things at any given moment. For instance, as you sit at home or at work and let your attention wander, you might notice some sounds from outside, a spot on the wall, a memory from last weekend, and a sense of comfort or discomfort from your clothes, all one after the other. As your attention drifts, one thing stands out and the others fade into the background or even disappear.

Sustained attention is called concentration. You use this when you are working at a task or on a project, watching a movie, or playing a game. In this kind of process your attention actually shifts quite a bit, but within a relatively narrow range.

In Huna there is a principle that says, "You get what you concentrate on." This means that the concentration of your attention sets up a vibration in your aura which will attract an experience related to what you are concentrating on. A fairly brief span of concentrated attention will usually produce only temporary and minor experiences. The longer the span of concentration and the more emotional energy put into it, the more long lasting and important are the experiences that are attracted, whether positive or negative. Like anything else, concentration on something can become a habit of thought or behavior. In that case the subconscious takes over the role of sustaining the concentration, reinforced by conscious attention. This is what produces the more or less permanent-seeming experiences of our lives. Such experiences will continue until we become aware of what we are doing and consciously change our focus of attention by the use of our will.

Conscious awareness is the totality of what is evident in the conscious mind at any given moment. It includes the experience of our physical senses and of mental events. Obviously we are not aware of *everything* that's going on in a particular moment. Things move in and out of awareness, and we have the ability to expand and contract our awareness, depending on what we are doing.

Attention and awareness are not the same, but neither can they be completely separated. You could say that attention is a tool of awareness. If you can imagine a lamp with a flashlight attached, awareness is like the lamp, which can light up a whole room, and attention is like the flashlight, which can bring out certain objects with more clarity. When awareness is limited (say to a single room), attention can be used to find a doorway to another room, thus permitting an expansion of awareness.

Both awareness and attention can be expanded or contracted, and it is probably true that most people simultaneously do both with each. When you watch a movie or read a book, the natural tendency is to get so involved (if it is good) that your awareness of anything else is greatly diminished or nonexistent. And, of course, this adds to the enjoyment. But a movie or book critic has to keep his attention on the story while at the same time being aware of other aspects like performance and style. A technique used in some martial arts is that of keeping attention on the opponent while being aware of the whole environment. Good drivers can engage in conversation and pay attention to the road while keeping part of their awareness on other cars and pedestrians. These examples are intended to show that you can focus attention and expand awareness at the same time, proving that they are not the same.

## VALUE FULFILLMENT

A secondary but very important attribute of the conscious mind is the urge toward value fulfillment. In other terms it is the urge toward finding and fulfilling purpose and meaning in life. To do this the conscious mind evaluates, i.e., it decides on the worth or value of things. While this is a necessary and useful attribute, it often gets distorted into making judgments of good or bad about everything. And that gets distorted into intolerance, injustice, and many other evils and ills. Some people will ponder on the meaning of life, and some will ponder on the meaning of a passing remark that someone just made to them. What matters is not only *what* you evaluate but *how* you evaluate.

As an example, self-improvement has a nice sound as a motivation for value fulfillment. However, because of individual interpretations or evaluations of its meaning and means, the effects are not always so nice. To very many, self-improvement means self-aggrandizement. All for one and one for oneself. Much of the misery in the world is due to this interpretation. Glory-seeking, greed, the hunger for control over others—all of these have the desire for self-improvement as their basis. At the same time there are those for whom self-improvement means helping others, bringing beneficial new ideas into manifestation, and increasing self-knowledge.

We are not given a meaning for our existence, nor do we have a built-in, fixed personal purpose. There is an overall purpose to each of our lives which is the responsibility of our Higher Selves, but that will be carried out regardless of what we do. Our personal purpose must be consciously decided upon, and we must create our own meaning for existence. The more this is in accord with the Higher Self, the more fulfilling it will be, though not necessarily easier. But value, meaning, and purpose, as they come into conscious awareness, must be decided upon consciously. The values and interpretations we give to the various experiences of life play the greatest role in determining our happiness and the quality of our life. The Huna guideline is to use love as a basis for evaluating everything, seeking always to create love where it seems to be lacking and to enhance it where it already exists.

### EFFORTLESS WILL

Just a final word on will power. We must realize that it doesn't take any effort to use our will. You have probably heard phrases like "He used a great effort of will to change his life." The source of the effort was not in the will but in the muscles of the body.

When people are trying to change a habit of thought or behavior, they often complain that it takes too much effort. Others may criticize them for not having a strong enough will. What actually happens is that such people are trying to force a habit to change by using their muscles against it, and this is true whether the habit is physical or mental. This kind of forceful attempt creates tension that locks up the body's energy and makes people feel worn out. They end up literally fighting themselves, which is rarely effective. All you really have to do is make your decision by your will, relax your muscles, and direct your attention in the way you want to go, until the new habit is established. If you ever feel that using your will is an effort, relax and start over.

# 5

## Getting to Know Your Subconscious

Your subconscious mind is a part of you. Yet it can seem like a perfect stranger if the ideas it operates by are quite different from the ideas that you consciously think you should operate by. Many people are so out of touch with their subconscious that it and their conscious mind can be likened to two businessmen who meet only to conduct the affairs of their company. They know nothing of each other's hopes and aspirations, likes and dislikes, fears, strengths, and weaknesses. Just as two businessmen who cooperate daily in certain respects may hold widely divergent political views, so may the conscious and subconscious hold widely different opinions in various things. The main difference, of course, is that the latter pair have to live together constantly, and conflicts are inevitable when they do not believe in the same things.

### BELIEFS OF THE SUBCONSCIOUS

The beliefs, attitudes, and opinions of the subconscious

54

are formed in early childhood for the most part. The religious, moral, and "life-coping" training received by the child from parental words and example can remain effective for a lifetime, unless changed by the conscious mind. The *lono* is well in the background during these early years and is not able to test and modify all the information received and stored by the *ku*. As the conscious mind grows in knowledge and experience, it can rationalize (test with common sense or logic) incoming data, so that less misinformation gets stored in the memory banks of the subconscious. But during childhood the subconscious accepts practically everything it receives as fact and acts accordingly. For instance, if a child is told repeatedly that he will catch a cold if his feet get wet, the *ku* will record that as a fact and make sure the body gets cold symptoms whenever the feet get wet. The *lono* may have learned in the meantime that there is no causal connection between wet feet and a cold. Still, unless the conscious adult knows how to communicate with his *ku*, he will catch a cold when he gets his feet wet because that is the belief held by the subconscious. In religious matters the divergence can be equally, if not more, important. It is almost a cliché to speak of the professed atheist who cries out for help to God when he is in mortal danger. The profession of atheism is done by the conscious mind, but the subconscious still believes in God. It is worse when fearful or misinterpreted religious beliefs interfere with one's proper enjoyment and fulfillment in life.

Many beliefs, attitudes, and opinions that are formed early in life simply change without any conscious effort, and many others are changed consciously with ease. Some, however, seemed locked in so tightly that even a hammer and chisel couldn't move them. This is only a problem when they give rise to behavior and experience that are unpleasant, painful, or dangerous.

In all cases where behavior and experience are difficult to change, it is because there are beliefs, attitudes, and opinions stored in the subconscious biocomputer that are held there by one or more powerful motivations. In spite of any negative behavior and experience that may be produced, the motivations are always positive. Your subconscious never works against *what it believes* are your best interests. Unfortunately, the assumptions on which those beliefs are based may be very faulty. For instance, if you grew up during the Great Depression and were exposed to the belief that rich people are all greedy, exploitive, snobbish, mean, and thoroughly disliked, then as an adult you might find yourself mysteriously unable to be financially successful, no matter what you do. In such a case your well-meaning *ku* may be trying to keep you from being greedy, exploitive, snobbish, mean, and thoroughly disliked. As another instance, if you grew up with religious training that drummed into you the idea that you were an unworthy sinner, you may as an adult find it nearly impossible to develop any degree of self-confidence or self-esteem. In that case your *ku* may be trying to protect you from offending God (and getting punished) because of the sin of pride.

If you are consciously aware of the beliefs held by your subconscious and the motivations that keep them operative, then you can use logic and alternative motivational strategies to make changes. The problem is that so many subconscious beliefs are "hidden" because they are too obvious to be noticed, because they are accepted as facts instead of beliefs, or because they are repressed from conscious awareness out of fear of the consequences of change. In order to develop fully and freely, you must know the contents of your own mind; you must "get to know your subconscious," for only then can you guide and enlighten it.

There are several ways to do this, and all require time and patience. Nothing worthwhile is achieved without effort, but effort can be pleasurable. In getting to know your subconscious you will discover a world of rich and varied beauty, as well as areas of darkness and pain. It is a journey for the brave, the adventurous, and the determined.

### NAME THAT KU

It is good Huna practice to give your subconscious a name. Since ancient times people have given personal names to concepts, forces, energies, things, and parts of things in order to establish rapport. In the case of your *ku*, just be careful that the naming doesn't establish a sense of separateness.

You can consciously choose to use your middle name, a made-up name, or the name of some favorite historical or fictional character. Max Long called his subconscious "George," after the phrase, "let George do it." Some people use "Subbie" and others are more inventive. You might try closing your eyes and saying, "All right, *ku*, what would you like to be called?" Then use the first name, if any, that pops into your mind.

This naming concept will be very useful in directing your subconscious to provide information and make changes, as well as in teaching it how to carry out instructions.

### MEMORY PROBE

There are two forms of searching your memory, both of which are best done in a comfortable position, either lying or sitting, in reasonably quiet surroundings. It is good to relax as much as you can, but you don't have to close your eyes.

The first form we will call "treasure hunt," the name given to it by Max Long. Start by talking to your subconscious as if it were a person, and tell it that you want to become better acquainted. Invite it to play a game with you. Name a memory of something pleasant that you wish to recall, and playfully challenge your *ku* to dig into the memory file and bring it back as quickly and in as much detail as possible. Or, as an

alternative, you might simply ask your subconscious
to bring up its own favorite memories. It may take
awhile at first, but once your *ku* catches on to what you
want, you will be in for some very interesting experiences. Memories of things you had entirely forgotten
will be replayed for you. Feelings and emotions of
long ago will come back, nearly as fresh as new. You may
even reexperience tactile sensations and odors, the smell
of fresh apple pie, for instance, or the feel of dry leaves
in autumn. You will learn a great deal about your subconscious, its likes and dislikes, as you continue this
exercise over a period of several days. The omission of
particular memories is also revealing. You may want
to relive a certain experience, but your *ku* will refuse to
bring it up. This may be the sign of a fear complex or
an important limiting belief in regard to the experience,
and should be noted for future investigation.

The second form we can call "trash collecting."
For this you have to be brave because you will be asking
your *ku* to bring up all its worst memories in full detail.
The objective here is to *be* objective, and to realize
that everything brought up is only stored information, including the feelings. After a little experience with
this, you will be able to notice one or more patterns
appearing. The memories will follow certain themes that
will provide you with clues to areas of limiting beliefs
that may be hampering your development. You may find,
for instance, that a whole series of "worst memories"
in a particular session has a fear-of-rejection theme
or a need-to-control theme. Watch for clues and keep
notes for study.

### Symbol Talk

Your subconscious communicates very well by
means of symbols, often better than with words
or memories. To use this method, you turn your attention
inward and think about some problem or an area of
your life you want to know more about. Then say "Give

me an image" or "Give me a symbol" for the thing you are asking about. The first image that comes to mind, no matter how bizarre or seemingly unrelated, is a symbolic message of how your *ku* relates to the situation. As an example, you may focus on a job situation and get an image of a torture chamber, which may be your *ku*'s way of expressing inner feelings about the job. It's up to you to interpret the symbols, and some people may find this easier than others. However, you can also ask the *ku* to give you another symbol if the first one is not clear enough. An important thing to remember is that these symbols only give you current feelings and beliefs held by the *ku*. Please don't make the mistake of thinking they are predictive, or you could scare yourself out of trying to make positive changes.

## BACKTALK

By providing a form that will make subconscious beliefs stand out more clearly, this method of *ku* communication takes advantage of the inner dialogue and/or argumentation that many people experience. All you do is turn your attention inward and repeat four statements slowly, three to five times each, leaving space between for any inner responses. The responses will usually come in the form of words, but sometimes there will be purely physical responses, or even images, either along with the words or alone.

Positive responses (encouraging words, good feelings or positive images) mean there is good subconscious support for what you want to do. Negative responses (criticism or argument, bad feelings, muscle tension, negative images, or no response of any kind) mean you have blocks to work through. If the backtalk is in words, you will have a better understanding of the specific beliefs involved. The four statements are:

1. I have the power (ability) to . . .
2. I have the right (I deserve) to . . .

3. I have the desire to . . .

4. I have the will (determination) to . . .

Fill in the blanks with your intent.

### IDEOMOTER RESPONSE

The ideomotor response involves the use of a simple instrument called a pendulum. This is a fairly quick and easy method of subconscious communication, once the *ku* has been trained and knows what is expected of it. The procedure is simply to take an object hanging from a piece of string or chain and hold it between the thumb and forefinger. Questions are then asked, and the pendulum will swing in response, often to the shocked surprise of the beholder.

Unfortunately, the use of a pendulum has been tainted with superstition, and people who like to think of themselves as scientifically minded are apt to reject the practice because of its association with spiritualism. This is because it has been claimed by the ignorant that disembodied spirits were moving the pendulum. I am not questioning the existence of disembodied spirits here, but only pointing out that such entities have nothing to do with the operation of the pendulum.

A more reasonable explanation is that the pendulum is moved by your own subconscious by means of very tiny muscular movements. These act upon the string or chain being held, and this motion is transferred to the weight, causing it to swing back and forth. It is no more mysterious than any other body functions carried out by the *ku*. The difference is that, in the case of the pendulum, the *ku* is allowed an opportunity to communicate directly with the conscious mind. The procedure is used by many psychoanalysts as a means of reaching the subconscious when all else has failed.

To begin the procedure, it is necessary to explain very carefully what you expect the *ku* to do. This is not as hard as it sounds. The subconscious is always awake. It reads what you read, hears what you hear, hears what you say, knows what you think. The problem is not how to get the *lono* to communicate with the *ku*, but the other way around. The explanation of the pendulum is best carried out by a combination of words and physical stimulus. Therefore, tell your subconscious that you are going to show it how to communicate with you. Draw a circle of about two inches in diameter upon a piece of paper. Make or buy a pendulum with a chain or string three to five inches long. If you want to make one, simply use a ring and a thread. Even car keys on a chain will do for a start. One of the first indications that your subconscious is an independent thinker may be its preference for one pendulum over another.

The next step is to set up a series of planned responses. You want your subconscious to be able to answer questions in a specific and consistent manner. "Yes" and "no" are the most important responses, but there are other possibilities as well. The ones to be given here are suggestive only.

You can start by holding the pendulum over the center of the circle you have drawn, preferably with your elbow resting on a table for support. Consciously move the pendulum in a clockwise circle, at the same time repeating to your subconscious aloud or silently that this response will mean "yes." Stop the pendulum and then swing it counterclockwise, repeating that this will mean "no." A back and forth swing crosswise to your body can mean "I don't want to answer," and an immobile pendulum can mean "I don't know" or "I don't understand the question." Remember that the direction of swings given here is optional, and you may wish to modify it to suit your taste. There is no universal response pattern.

After demonstrating to your subconscious what you want it to do, try the method by holding the pendulum motionless over the circle and asking questions to which you already know the answer. Do not try to prevent the pendulum from moving, but do not consciously try to make it move either. If you aren't sure whether you are consciously making it move, then you probably aren't. In operation the movement may begin slowly and gradually increase in the size of the swing, but it will not be as strong as a conscious movement unless the question also releases a lot of emotion. The fingers and hand may not seem to move at all, or there may be very slight but visible twitchings and jerks. Be sure to bring the pendulum to a complete stop between questions in order not to mistake inertia for answers.

For most people the response will be immediate. It is as if the subconscious has been anxiously waiting for an opportunity to communicate. However, some people may get no response to begin with. If this happens it is usually because the *ku* did not fully understand the instructions, or because there may be some fear of using the pendulum. The solution for this is patient repetition and expressing confidence that only the muscles are involved, until the message gets across. In fairly rare cases consistent lack of response may be an indication that the *lono* and *ku* are at serious odds with each other. In such instances other methods will have to be tried.

Another type of response is the pendulum moving erratically, without regard to the pattern set. The subconscious may be playing games and will eventually settle down to the proper responses. Or it may be signaling that a different set of responses will be better. If the subconscious continues to play, a demonstration by another person will often help to straighten it out. Should that fail, other methods of communication will have to be tried until the *ku* has more respect for the *lono*.

Once a positive response has been obtained, you can begin to ask questions that will lead to a better understanding of your subconscious. The beginner will

naturally wonder how accurate the responses will
be. Experience among many people has shown a high
rate of accuracy, subject, of course, to the nature
and clarity of the question. The subconscious takes
things literally, so a question must be free of ambiguity
in order to avoid an ambiguous answer. When you get an
answer that seems inaccurate, or if you get an "I don't
want to answer" response, rephrase the question
several times. Don't be surprised if you get an answer
you don't like, for you may have been avoiding that
knowledge. Don't be surprised either if you get an
answer that simply confirms what you know and believe
consciously. After all, you are questioning a part of
your own mind.

As to the types of questions to ask, they are only
limited by your imagination, the response pattern, and
the information which the subconscious can reasonably
be expected to have. Questions about your state of
mental and physical health can be very informative.
Religious beliefs held by the *ku* can be explored, as can
its attitudes toward other people. The *ku* may show a
dislike for people you consider as friends and a liking for
people you try to avoid. Further questioning can un-
cover the reasons. Many people use a pendulum to
determine which foods the subconscious prefers for the
body, or what nutrients might be lacking. Another
very useful line of questioning has to do with dream
interpretation. The symbolism of dreams may be strange
to the *lono*, but the *ku* knows the inner meaning. After a
few weeks of using the pendulum, you will be amazed
at the rich source of information you have within.

Some people, however, get carried away with this
process and expect too much from the *ku*. Questions
about the future, for instance, are no more accurate
than they would be if you made an intelligent guess.
The subconscious is by no means omniscient. Another
aberration is to start depending on your *ku* for all
decision-making. It can tell you how it feels about a

situation and may even make a recommendation, but this ought to be weighed like any advice from a good friend. The decision is the responsibility of the *lono*. Remember that the object of all this is to get to know your subconscious, not to make it into a god.

# 6

# The Reality of the Invisible

One of the more important concepts in Huna is that of *aka*. Dictionary definitions for this word include "shadow; reflection, likeness, image; essence as opposed to substance; clarity, brightness; embryo; and transparent." The closest concepts in English would be the ether, etheric or astral matter, and the aura. The idea of the ether connotes an invisible sort of "prematter" which connects and penetrates everything in the physical universe and which serves as the medium for energy effects. This concept has gone in and out of popularity among scientists, and the idea of an aura and etheric or astral bodies is definitely outside the belief systems of most of the scientific community.

Until quite recently, the existence of *aka* was dependent on the witness of clairvoyants and psychics who claimed to be able to see or feel the *aka* body surrounding the physical one when the conditions were right. Some said that they could also see or feel the *aka* around inanimate objects and plants, and a few even professed to be able to create independent objects or entities of pure *aka* that could be seen or felt by anyone. And, of course, there were those who could see the *aka* bodies of people who had passed on and/or the forms of "nature spirits" or other beings. Since these effects were not measurable or reproducible in the laboratory, scientists scoffed and paid no attention to them. There were brave exceptions, but their views carried no weight in the scientific community.

Then a Russian couple named Kirlian recorded very odd phenomena when high voltages were passed through animate and inanimate objects lying on a photographic plate. A hazy, blue corona appeared around the objects, or at least around their image on the plate. More experiments showed that the corona's shape, size, and color varied with the health and emotional states of individuals and the state of decay of plant cuttings. People with apparent healing abilities were found to have larger coronas, sometimes tinged with red, and "ghost" coronas appeared where parts of leaves had been cut off. Most scientists agree now that these photographic effects are caused by electrical changes, but the mystery of what causes the changes in the object photographed remains a mystery. Some people feel that it reflects changes in the aura or *aka* body.

As more scientists began to explore the Kirlian phenomena, they came across the writings and research of those few scientists who had dared to explore this area before them. Among these were Baron von Reichenbach in the nineteenth century, inventor of creosote, who discovered many visual and tactile properties of *aka*; Dr. Kilner, a physician in England who during the early part of this century discovered a means of viewing the aura for diagnostic purposes; Dr. Wilhelm Reich, who discovered many properties of *aka*, including the blue color so often apparent, and who measured its effects with a geiger counter and an electroscope; and Dr.

Harold Burr, a contemporary of Reich, who succeeded in measuring the electrical field around living things with a voltmeter.

Many people can see *aka*, and its interaction with electricity apparently can be recorded. It is real. At the end of this chapter I will give you some experiments that you can do yourself to experience it.

### FIELD CHARACTERISTICS

Before discussing the specific characteristics of *aka* itself, a distinction must be made between energy and the medium through which that energy manifests. Just as water and copper wire serve as mediums for electricity, so *aka* serves as a medium for the life energy, *mana*. When you see the aura, you are seeing a field of *aka* charged with *mana* or, to put it another way, you are seeing the effects of a *mana* charge on *aka* substance. Sometimes it is convenient to speak only of the energy itself, as Reich did in his orgone work, but sometimes the *aka* must be taken into account for understanding and practice.

First let's consider field effects. I have already mentioned the aura, which the kahunas called *kahoaka*. Think of it not just as something that surrounds you, but as a field which serves as the matrix for your body. For practical purposes, then, we can speak of an *aka* body that both penetrates and surrounds (or extends beyond) the physical body. During sleep and at other times, by accident or mastery, a major portion of this *aka* body can disengage from the physical and travel, with or without consciousness on the part of the person involved. Some kind of link is retained between the traveling *aka* body and the physical one. This is often perceived as a "silver cord" by those who are out of the body. Sensory information flows through this contact, so that at any sign of trouble or discomfort at either end, the *kahoaka* comes zipping back, frequently causing the physical body to jerk when it does so.

67

Another field effect is that of changing the size, density, and energy capacity of the *aka* body through emotion, imagination, and/or intent. Any strong emotion will usually increase the size and brightness of the aura. On the other hand, emotional suppression and illness will usually decrease the aura's size and brightness. These same effects, however, can be achieved by conscious intent with the help of imagination. By the same process you can change the density of the field, so that in one moment a group of people can barely lift you, and in the next they find you almost as light as a feather. It is also possible to learn how to expand the aura and thereby extend your senses of sight, hearing, and touch into more distant parts of your immediate environment.

The *aka* field serves as well for the storage of memory. Traditional scientists claim that thoughts are recorded on the physical brain cells, though no trace of such recording has ever been found. Much has been made of the fact that electrodes stimulating certain parts of the brain have evoked vivid memories, but the same memories can be evoked by stimulating other parts of the brain and even other parts of the body. In Huna theory, every thought does produce a corresponding cellular change, *which may be changed again* by the next thought. This would explain why no permanent trace can be found for memory. The thought itself (and this applies to experience, too) is actually recorded on *aka* substance, and the subconscious taps this source for memory. It is for this reason that we can recall past lives, dreams, imagining, visions, and other forms of inner experience that have no physical counterpart.

The storage function of the *aka* field permits us to pick up or tune into memories that are personal as well as those which we have no direct connection with. Perhaps you have heard of the "Akashic Records," a concept from India that has been distorted in the West. First, note the root *aka* in *Akashic*. The original Indian concept is identical to that of Huna. All events, including thoughts, are recorded by or impressed upon *aka* substance. With the right focus of mind, it is possible to tune into everything that has ever been thought, felt, said, or done. Because of our intimate connection and concern with our physical self, and because of our cultural conditioning, we find it easy and natural to be more aware of personal memories from this lifetime, but there are sensitives and psychics who dip into other kinds of memory on a more or less regular basis.

### TRANSMISSION CHARACTERISTICS

As the medium for energy transmission, *aka* is used to communicate information and experience from one point to another. In this section we will be concerned with only the psychic aspects of this phenomenon.

In Huna there are currently two main working theories for the operation of psychic reception and influence. The first, popularized by Max Long, uses the analogy of *aka* threads, cords, and fingers and ignores the existence of the general *aka* field. According to this analogy, we remain in contact with everything we sense by means of "sticky" *aka* threads, like drawn out strands of bubble gum, that never break and never get tangled. Every time we renew contact, another thread is formed, so that we are connected to certain people and places by cords rather than threads. In addition, by the power of thought we have the ability to send out an *"aka* finger" to places or people we have never been in contact with, and thereby seek out information or have an influence. Still within the analogy, it is said that the subconscious sends out a portion of our sensing ability to record impressions or make something happen. Telepathy, then, is a matter of "activating" a particular thread with *mana* to send or receive through it; clairvoyance of sending out a "finger" to observe; and psychokinesis of making the finger strong enough to move something.

In practical experience, the analogy is somewhat useful for beginners but inherently limiting. For instance, it breaks down completely in the area of radionics, where the theoretical position that destroying a photographic negative breaks the link between the subject and his photo is demonstrably not true. The idea of threads, cords, and fingers has its uses, but should not be applied as dogma.

The second main working theory conceives the *aka* as an all-pervasive etheric substance that serves as a perfect conductor for energy radiation of all kinds. The analogy is that of sound, light, or heat radiating out in all directions from a point of origin and being perceived or influenced by whatever is attuned to the right frequency.

This theory also incorporates the concept of radio waves and electromagnetism. In this analogy the mind is the tuner, and *mana* is the energy that powers it. The more *mana* you have, the better your ability to receive or transmit. Telepathy, then, becomes a matter of tuning in to the thought broadcasting of a particular person; clairvoyance of tuning in to the radiations of a particular area; and psychokinesis of adjusting your energy transmission to produce an induction effect on a particular object. This theory treats past events as vibrations or frequency patterns still actively transmitting through the *aka* at a rate too slow to perceive without normal senses, and future events are vibrations moving too fast to perceive normally.

In practice this theory is extremely useful and effective, but it requires a technical way of thinking that is difficult for some people to work with. The analogy of sound is probably the best way to introduce the theory.

As an aside, one might ask, "Why not go straight to the truth, rather than dealing with working theories and analogies?" The question assumes that there is one absolute truth behind all the appearances and theories. In Huna we don't assume that at all. The only acceptable definition of absolute truth would be "all that is, was, will be, and could possibly be anywhere and anywhen." With such an assumption, truth in practical terms is what you make it, what you decide it is, and effective truth is what works best for the task at hand.

### MATERIALIZATION CHARACTERISTICS

*Aka* is not only the all-pervasive ether that records events and transmits energy; it is also the matrix of all physical form. Kahunas teach that a thought-image radiating into the general *aka* field produces several effects, depending on the clarity, energy-intensity, and duration of the thought. It may manifest as an invisible thought form, seen only by certain sensitives, if at all; it may manifest as a visible thought form of temporary duration, often mistaken for a departed spirit; it may, while invisible, serve as a focus for attracting the materials and circumstances necessary for bringing its physical equivalent into personal experience; and it may manifest on the spot from etheric to physical, with as much duration as anything else in the physical world. There are many variations of the above, but those are the general effects.

In daydreaming or fantasizing, the persons and objects visualized are in truth products of the imagination—material products formed out of *aka* substance. Usually they break up into unformed *aka* once the daydreaming session is over, but their duration is actually determined by the amount of *mana* they receive. The more often something is visualized, the more energy it receives through the very process of visualization. In ordinary daydreaming without a lot of emotion, the amount of energy received by the image each time is very small; but over a period of years of visualizing the same thing, the *aka* thought form gradually has an increasing effect on one's life, even if the physical equivalent is never manifested in any way. You might think of these images as floating in your personal *aka* field where they

subconsciously influence your perspective of life,
your reactions, and the reactions of other people to you.

*Aka* thought forms can vary in size from microscopic
to as large as you can imagine. In terms of images, the
smallest ones appear to exist in your "mind's eye." You
think of a scene or a person, and picture the object
interiorly. In effect, it is very much like memory recall,
and such thought forms are, in fact, recorded as memory,
even though they may bear no relation to actual physical
experience.

Somewhat different in size and effect are exteriorized
*aka* images constructed by the conscious mind. This is
the type of visualization used in pantomime, for
instance. According to Huna theory, what you experience because of the mime's gestures is not just
imagined. The performer visualizes life-sized objects
right there on the stage and handles them or inter-
acts with them as if they were real. The audience sees
nothing, but if the performer has done a good job of
visualization, his reactions will be so realistic that the
audience will know exactly what is being portrayed
because they will have created similar *aka* images of their
own. Certain kinds of Chinese and Japanese paintings
are similar to pantomime in that they merely suggest
many elements of a scene and leave it to the viewer's
imagination to fill in the rest of it. The viewer con-
structs an exteriorized *aka* thought form to do the filling
in, and it can be very interesting to compare the details
filled in by different viewers.

Under hypnosis people can be led to see themselves in completely different surroundings and to carry
on conversations with persons who are not really there.
For the hypnotized subject they *are* there, in the form of
*aka* images created by the subject himself.

There are cases on record of mass hallucination
where a whole crowd of wide-awake people has wit-
nessed an event that did not objectively occur. In one
such instance, an Indian fakir performed the famous rope

trick. A large crowd saw the rope fly up into the air and hang there while a small boy climbed up and disappeared. The fakir climbed up after him, threw down bloody pieces of the boy's body, climbed down, and made the boy whole again. However, a movie camera recording the event showed only the fakir and the boy standing quietly next to a limp length of rope the whole time. What happened? The fakir had constructed *aka* images of himself, the boy, and the rope that were so dense that they could be seen by everyone present, but so fine that the camera could not record them. In a sense the fakir was a faker, but in another sense he demonstrated a tremendous mastery over *aka*.

EXPERIMENTS

1. *Seeing aka*: The simplest way to see *aka* is to hold your hand with fingers spread about two or three inches above a plain dark or light surface. If you use a light surface, make sure there is no shadow directly under your hand. Black felt is ideal as a background surface. When your hand is in place, focus your gaze between your fingers and just over the fingertips, on the space itself and not on the background or your hand. Right away, or in a few moments, you will see a fairly faint and hazy outline of light around your fingers. This is the denser part of your *aka* field. If you look beyond your fingers six inches or more and then back again, you will be able to see the contrasting haze around your fingers more clearly.

Another way to see *aka* is to have a friend sit against a blank wall in dim light with no shadows. You can then gaze just above his or her head. A similar haze will become visible around your friend's head and/or shoulders.

2. *Feeling aka*: Your *aka* field is easier to feel when it is charged with energy. A simple way to feel it is to rub your palms together for a few moments (which stimulates the release of *mana* from your hands) and then hold

your palms about six inches to a foot apart. Next bring your hands toward each other *very* slightly, back and forth, several times. It will feel somewhat like you are gently squeezing a soft balloon. In any case there will be a definite sensation of something invisible resisting the motion of your hands. This is the *aka*. When you get more sensitive, you won't have to rub your hands to feel it, and you can go on to feeling the aura around people's bodies and eventually inanimate objects as well.

By practicing the awareness of *aka* you will be increasing your sensitivity to finer sensory input from your subconscious, and this kind of communication will be valuable for your self-development.

# 7

# Mana, Mysterious Energy of Life

*Mana* is the energy behind all life and a potential source of incredible power. Yet it has been ignored by conservative Western scientists, although discovered time and time again by those more daring and open-minded.

Franz Anton Mesmer discovered it in the eighteenth century and gave it the name of animal magnetism (not to be confused with the same term used by Christian Scientists). As an example of how threatening his discovery was, Mesmer's name today is associated only with hypnotism, a byproduct of his work with the vital force.

About fifty years after Mesmer, Baron von Reichenbach investigated the claims for this force, proved its existence by many experiments, and called it odic force. In spite of his reputation as the inventor of creosote, however, Reichenbach's discovery was ignored or scorned by most other scientists of his time.

Freud suggested existence of this force and called

it "libido," and a doctor named Abrams investigated
its bioelectric characteristics. Wilhelm Reich, a protegé
of Freud's, made more discoveries about it, did extensive experiments with it, wrote books about it, and
invented devices to generate it. The U. S. Govern-
ment sent him to jail, burned his books, and confiscated
his devices. Reich's name for vital force was "orgone
energy."

A Frenchman, Bovis, discovered this force in pyra-
mids, and later scientists in several Eastern Bloc nations
experimented with it under the name of "psycho-
tronic energy." Meanwhile, and for centuries past, other
cultures familiar with this energy have given it names
like *prana, baraka, mungo, ch'i,* and *ki,* to mention a few.
The term I will use is *mana,* from Polynesia, and in
this chapter the emphasis will be on its biological aspect.

## EBB AND FLOW

*Mana* is the energy that gives you life—your "life
force." One of the main characteristics of life as we know
it is movement, expressed in such ways as blood circulation, the digestive process, and electrical activity
of the nervous system. The Huna theory is that all these
life processes are made possible by the continuous
movement of *mana* through and around the body. A very
good analogy is that the *mana* flowing through the body
is like an electrical current, and the *mana* flowing
around the body is like a magnetic field. An increase in
one will increase the other, and a depletion in one
will deplete the other. Also, various environmental influences can cause fluctuations in both the current and
field, with resulting effects on health, mood, and
thoughts. Personal behavior, emotional habits, and
mental attitudes can affect the ebb and flow of *mana*
as well.

When your flow of *mana* is strong and clear, you
are at your peak of physical health; you have abundant
energy and strength; you can remain calm or enthusiastic

under trying conditions; you can think clearly and effectively; you have great confidence and compassion; you feel happy; and your physical and psychic abilities are most efficient. When your flow is low and constricted, you will be in poor health; you will feel weak and tired; you will be irritable and/or anxious under trying conditions; your thinking will be muddled; you will have a lack of confidence and little empathy; you will be very unhappy; and your abilities will be hard to express. Now these are the extremes, of course, and while many people may experience them at one time or another, most of the time most people are in a mixed state in which some parts of their life are flowing and some parts are at an ebb.

Let's look at the major factors that affect the ebb and flow of the life force.

### DIET

After living in different parts of the world and experimenting with many kinds of diets, I have become convinced that, in terms of life energy, it doesn't matter *what* you eat. What does matter most is the following:

> the quality of the food;
> your state of stress when you eat it;
> the focus of your attention.

Quality of food includes its nutritional value, its freshness, its method of preparation, and its appearance/ odor (the latter for its effect on your mind). Whether the food is fish, fowl, meat, or vegetables is insignificant except at a personal belief level, although under certain conditions it may be beneficial physically to restrict one or more types of food. As important as quality is, however, it is definitely secondary to the other two factors.

If you eat under stress (mental, emotional, or physical) you will not only get less nutritional benefit from any food you eat, but in the process of converting the food to energy, your body may also convert some of it to toxins. This will increase your stress and further deplete your life force.

Eating mechanically—i.e., while your attention and awareness are almost fully on something else like reading, T.V., or conversation—will result in poor absorption of nutrients and/or more conversion of the food energy to fat. This means less *mana* flow for daily use. I am not advocating complete concentration on your food when you eat, though that would be the most beneficial and could actually produce a "high." I do recommend reserving at least a part of your attention and awareness for tasting and enjoying the food, whatever else you are doing.

A fourth important factor—which is too involved for discussion here, but which definitely affects the *mana* you get from eating—is your attitude toward the foods you eat and toward the process of eating itself.

### BREATHING

Breathing is even more necessary to staying alive than eating. There are cases of people remaining alive and healthy without eating, but absolutely none of people who have done so without breathing. On the physical level breathing introduces oxygen into the lungs, which makes it possible for cells to utilize the nutrients in the bloodstream. According to Huna, the *mana* current and field are also strengthened in this process.

Because of its importance, breath has been used as a symbol for life and the life force itself in many cultures, and some have developed numerous techniques for consciously regulating the breathing process in order to increase or direct *mana*. However, proper breathing is really a very simple matter. A common bad habit in this country, often the result of chronic stress, is shallow breathing, in which people use only a small portion of their lungs to take in air and thus deprive themselves of one of the best sources of life energy. As simple a technique as inhaling fully and exhaling completely will have remarkable effects on your health and clarity of thought, if you have been breathing shallowly. Deep breathing will also help to calm you if you tend to be nervous and give you more energy if you tend to be tired.

Perhaps the best form of deep breathing is a Yoga technique known as the Complete Breath, also used in Huna. Begin by exhaling completely all the air in your lungs. Push it all out by forcing your upper abdomen inward. You should be able to put your hand on this area and feel it sinking toward your spine. Then let the air come down into the bottom of your lungs, and feel it force your upper abdomen outward. When that area has reached the limit of expansion, continue to inhale, filling up the top of your lungs as well. When your chest is fully expanded, let the air out of the top of your lungs first, and then push out the rest by contracting your abdomen. One cycle of inhaling and exhaling in this manner is known as the Complete Breath. Don't count the first exhalation; it is only a good way to get the cycle started. The breathing should be slow and easy. Four Complete Breaths are enough for one session until it becomes natural for you. Doing this as a regular practice will help to vitalize every area of your life.

#### ATTITUDES

Mental and emotional attitudes can either inhibit or enhance the flow of *mana* in your being. Generally speaking, negative attitudes produce inner stress, which translates as physical tension and can affect organs and even cells. It is this tension that directly inhibits your flow of *mana*. When attitudes are involved and remain unchanged, any physical attempt to get your flow going (such as super vitamins, exercise, or special breathing) will usually just give temporary results, although increasing the flow of *mana* in some people will result in a change of attitude as well.

The most direct way to improve *mana* flow is to change negative attitudes to positive ones, especially those having to do with fear, doubt, resentment, and guilt. In developing a more positive attitude, it is important that you learn not to be afraid of negative thoughts and feelings that may come up from time to time. It doesn't matter if they appear; just be aware of them and chase them out. It does matter if you let them hang around. The most direct and simple way to change a negative attitude to a positive one is to be aware of the negative thoughts or feelings when they come up and consciously change them to their positive opposites. You can do this whether or not the apparent facts of the situation seem to warrant it. If you practice this consistently, you will be amazed at how your life, including health and energy, will begin to improve at all levels.

### VISUALIZATION

Visualization may be used to enhance *mana* flow at any level of need for any purpose. Here I am going to tell you how to use it for building up a "supercharge" of *mana*. This is best done by a combination of deep breathing, visualization, and a physical stimulus. It is useful for those who want to get into the range of "high health," exceptional accomplishment, or mind expansion.

At least four deep breaths should be taken while giving a mental command to your subconscious to accumulate a high charge of *mana*. As you breathe deeply, visualize yourself being filled with energy. You can imagine it coming into you through the top of your head in the form of a beam from the sun or the stars; as a surrounding cloud which is absorbed into you; as an energized liquid that fills your body like a cup; or in any way that makes you feel that something is happening. The visualization serves as a plan for your subconscious and emphasizes the command word or phrase. In deciding on a visualization to use, you have to take into account the likes and dislikes of your subconscious. You must discover what is most effective for your *ku*, because the effect is more important than the image.

The purpose of the physical stimulus is to convince your *ku* that you mean business. Deep breathing by itself will give you a fair increase in *mana*, but you want an extra large increase. Until you have trained your *ku* well, it may take your visualization as just another daydream. A physical stimulus, however, impresses your *ku* with a greater sense of reality, and its response is vital to your success. Light physical exercise such as a few jumping jacks or briefly running in place might do the trick, and so can a "moving meditation" like T'ai Ch'i Ch'uan. Of course, physical movement isn't necessary at all. You could hold a special object, do a special ritual, go to a special place—as long as you do something physical that you associate with increasing *mana*.

I suggest that you use the physical stimulus just before or along with the breathing and visualization. After a certain amount of repetition of this combination, you should be able to drop the physical stimulus and accumulate your supercharge by breathing and visualization alone, under any conditions in any place. If your visualization is good enough so that you can imagine something physical as if it were real, then you can eliminate the stimulus in the first place.

### EFFECTS OF ACCUMULATING MANA

While practicing the accumulation of *mana*, be alert for any physical sensations that might occur. Specifically, you might feel a tingling in some part of your body, perhaps your hands, solar plexus, or the center of your forehead. You may also feel a kind of current running up or down the center of your body or along your spine. This is perfectly normal and only means your psychoenergetic sensitivity is increasing. For those of you

familiar with Kundalini Yoga, the raising of the fire
from the base of the spine is the same as the process of
accumulating extra *mana.*

Another effect of a large accumulation of *mana* could
be a feeling of weightlessness or even spinning. If this
bothers you, keep your eyes open until you get used
to it. *Mana* has antigravity or levitative properties, so the
sense of weightlessness can be real. Naturally, it acts
first on your *aka* body, the lightest part of you, so there
may not be an actual physical change in weight. The
Spanish mystic, St. Theresa, was one of many who have
experienced actual levitation.

Some effects of *mana* can be seen with the naked
eye, once your sensitivity begins to increase. In a
darkened room, after having accumulated an extra supply of *mana,* focus your eyes on the air about a foot or
two in front of your body. If your eyes have become
sensitive enough, you will see what appears to be rising
heat waves all around you. The phenomenon will have a
"ghostly" appearance, but do not be misled into thinking you are seeing spirits. It is merely an effect of *mana.*
The visible aura is another effect of *mana,* as are the
dancing lights that are sometimes seen. *Mana* can be
felt with your hands, too, as discussed in chapter 6.

### MANA AND PSI PHENOMENA

All Huna practices use *mana* as the energy to power
them. In telepathy, for instance, the more energy you
put into a projected thought, the better chance it will
have of reaching its target, and the clearer it will be.
Energy is not the same as desire or will. It is simply the
amount of life force available.

In very practical terms, *mana* is directly related
to emotion. The greater the inner excitement, the greater
the supply of *mana,* and the more effective the practices
will be. This is true for healing, traveling clairvoyance,
projection, protection, or any other practice. You do
not have to be consciously concerned with how the

subconscious is going to use the *mana* to do what you want, any more than you have to consciously concern yourself with the process of digestion or cell regeneration. The subconscious knows how to do it. The *ku* merely needs to be told what to do and be convinced that it is able to do it.

A very large supply of *mana* is needed to produce effects like psychokinesis, the moving of objects without physical means. It has been noted that poltergeist phenomena occur most frequently in the presence or proximity of a child going through puberty, that stage of life when new body centers are coming to life and the *mana* flows more abundantly. In such cases, however, the adolescent is almost always emotionally frustrated, which causes the *mana* to dam up and then burst forth with a tremendous discharge of pure power. Spirits have nothing to do with this. It is just raw energy. Usually this ability disappears as the child's body metabolism becomes more stable and frustrations are cleared up. It is entirely possible for an adult to learn how to move objects with *mana*, but it may be difficult because of the necessity of accumulating an exceptional supply of *mana* and keeping it under control, and the necessity of convincing the subconscious that the effort is worthwhile.

*Mana* can be accumulated and stored and then released slowly or all at once. As natural as air and water, as versatile as electricity and magnetism, *mana* will simply keep you alive, or it can change your life. It's your decision to make.

83

# 8

# Clearing the Path to Power

Your door to power—the power to create your own reality freely and enjoyably—is constructed of your beliefs about what is and is not humanly possible. What blocks that door and keeps you from going through it, even when you believe something is possible, is a special set of beliefs, attitudes, and behaviors that we call a "complex." Thanks to popular presentations of psychology, the idea of complexes which hinder a person's effectiveness is not a strange one. Freud is generally given credit for their discovery, but the ancient kahunas knew about them for many thousands of years before he was born. They not only knew about complexes, but knew more about them and devised far more effective ways of dealing with them.

## UNDERSTANDING COMPLEXES

The word "complex" comes from Latin and means "closely connected, or a weaving and twining together." In psychoanalysis specifically it refers to a group of emotional attitudes which are partly unconscious and which affect the behavior of an individual. The Hawaiian language has quite a number of words that refer to complexes, most of which use roots that have the meaning of "a web."

In saying that emotional attitudes comprise a complex, we are really saying that they are part of the *ku* or subconscious. The complex is a group of ideas or attitudes about a certain subject which the subconscious believes to be true. In this broad sense our beliefs about God, country, love, money can all be considered complexes. When we ask a person, "How do you feel about money?" we are asking him to describe the intricate complex of beliefs built up through teaching and experience in regard to that subject. It is significant that we use the word *feel*, a word which represents the domain of the *ku*.

We know that the subconscious records everything that happens to us in its memory bank, and that all the impressions surrounding a particular event or object are linked together by the *ku*, so that it can recall them to present a complete memory of the event or object. Abstract concepts such as love also form a sort of center around which experiences, teachings, and impressions are gathered in the memory bank for storage and recall. The way you feel about love, for instance, depends on the kinds of experiences, teachings, and other impressions related to love that your *ku* piles up on the basic concept. In a healthy situation your understanding of the concept grows as you receive more data input. Each new experience is added to the rest, ideally producing a new synthesis each time.

Unfortunately, a normally growing complex of ideas and attitudes occasionally becomes fixed, frequently at an early age. When this happens, there is no more growth, no increased understanding. New experiences and teachings which do not conform to the fixed complex are shunted aside to an unrelated storage area. A person with such a complex may have radically different memories concerning a particular topic, but the set comprising the complex is the only one he ever voluntarily remembers. The other memories exist in limbo somewhere. An outstanding example is a complex of racial prejudice. The person brought up to firmly believe that another race is inferior to his may apparently remain blind all his life to thousands of examples to the contrary. Or he may intellectually accept equality but emotionally be unable to deal with it.

What causes a complex to become fixed? One thing is a shock which occurs when the conscious mind is not in a position to rationalize or make the experience acceptable in terms of what is already known. An example is the baby who is frightened by a furry animal and who may thereafter be frightened by anything furry, even bearded men. Another type of complex (I will use the term now to mean a fixed complex) which occurs under shock can take place when a person is knocked unconscious. The conscious mind is out of the way, but the *ku* is still active. Let us suppose, for instance, that a young man is knocked unconscious, and a bystander mentions to a friend that the young man no doubt has suffered brain damage. It is possible that the young man's *ku* would accept that assertion as fact and cause the young man on awakening to act as if indeed he did have brain damage, perhaps for the rest of his life, even if nothing were wrong.

Far more common than shock in promoting the formation of complexes is repetition of an idea by an authority, especially when that repetition evokes a strong emotion such as fear. Many complexes having to do with religion and sin are established in this way. When a person, especially a young person, is threatened with damnation if he strays from the path decreed by someone accepted as a representative of God, then a complex about the decree is almost sure to develop.

Complexes are lodged in the subconscious. In many

cases we do not become consciously aware of them until an occasion arises which threatens the fixed beliefs. In this way you can see that a complex is really a kind of habit which operates only when circumstances call it forth.

However, there does exist a type of complex which is formed and held by the conscious mind itself. In this case the conscious mind conceives the belief and cooperates fully with the subconscious in maintaining it. We might take as an example the belief in a political party or a scientific theory. These beliefs may be strenuously held in the face of overwhelmingly opposing evidence. Most likely, it is an intense feeling of insecurity that gives rise to conscious complexes. The complexed belief represents something solid to hang onto.

Fixed complexes are not all necessarily harmful. A complex about catching a cold if you sit in a draft is not going to hurt anyone, though it may cause a lot of colds. A complex about smoking causing cancer may even be helpful. It is when a complex begins to impair our effectiveness as human beings, or acts to prevent our spiritual growth, that we are in danger. An inferiority complex has a severely inhibiting effect. A belief that one is being persecuted by others can lead to self-destruction. Complexes that involve hate and fear, obsessions and compulsions, can get one into all sorts of trouble.

### FEAR AND GUILT COMPLEXES

Perhaps the most destructive and inhibiting kind of complex is known generically as the guilt complex. This is a fixed belief that you are guilty of something and that you deserve to be punished. In its worst form it includes the idea that what you did was so bad that you are unworthy of forgiveness.

The guilt complex is a reaction of the *ku* to the individual's noncompliance with some other complex.

Most often it is connected with religious beliefs about sin. In other cases there may be guilt over a breach of ethics, as when someone has ruined another person financially, even though the operation was strictly legal.

When the guilt is shared by the conscious mind, the guilt will generally take an outward form. A person who knowingly feels guilty about being extremely selfish in one area of life may try to punish himself or compensate by being over generous in another area. Sharp business practices often lead to generous donations to charities, and parents who are selfish with time may be generous with cash, gifts, and privileges.

When guilt feelings are not conscious, they can give rise to neurotic behavior and psychosomatic illness. Since psychosomatic ailments comprise a very high percentage of all illnesses, we can determine that hidden guilt feelings must be very prevalent, even if we assume that not all of the illnesses are caused by guilt per se. The neuroses or illnesses caused by guilt are most often a form of self-punishment inflicted by the *ku* in order to ward off some worse punishment by Mommy or Daddy or God.

On the same order of seriousness as guilt complexes, and sometimes intertwined with them, are fear complexes which prevent a person from engaging in certain activities or following certain lines of study. These, too, often have their roots in early childhood training. Because Huna includes knowledge that was once, and in some circles still is, considered taboo, it is not uncommon for someone to begin a study of Huna and then drop it at the urging of the subconscious. The information presented or the experiences had come in conflict with complexed beliefs. Such a person will be stunted in his spiritual and psychic growth and subject to the dictates of other people's beliefs unless he can train his *ku* to be open minded enough to study, compare, exercise, and then make a judgment based on fact. No knowledge, even that of Huna, should ever be accepted

on blind faith, nor should it ever be rejected without
consideration.

An unhealthy complex can be recognized by the
effects it produces when threatened. All sudden illnesses
should be examined to see whether they prevent you
from doing something which may be against the
principles or beliefs you hold or may have held at one
time. Of course, the effects of some complexes may be so
displaced (i.e., their source is so disguised) that the
reason behind them cannot be recognized, at least not
by superficial analysis. Others have their effect over
such a long period of time that their recognition is also extremely difficult. The easiest complex to recognize is
that which produces an unreasonable emotional reaction, frequently in the fields of politics, religion, and
science.

## COMPLEX ENERGY

Emotion is a subconscious function. It is a release
of energy programmed in a particular way by the *ku*.
Psychosomatic illness, on the other hand, seems to be a
programmed blockage of energy at or to the affected
part. In fact, the complex itself is held together by
energy or *mana*. It is obvious that *mana* blockages
diminish our effectiveness in the outer world. Not so
obvious is the fact that they also restrict or prevent our
spiritual growth and use of psychic abilities. We need
*mana* to carry out both of these. If most of it is bound up
in complexes, we have that much less to use psychically
and spiritually. Also the complex, either of guilt or
fear, may be specifically programmed to block such use.
One very sad effect of this is that the *ku* may refuse
to cooperate in prayer or meditation, because of complexes involving feelings of unworthiness or fear of loss
of control.

Psychically, the less *mana* generated, the less
accurate or effective one will be, since all psi phenomena
are dependent on energy. If the *ku* has been

89

indoctrinated with a strong fear of the unknown or
a fear of psychic phenomena as such, it will block the
door to power. This does not mean that the person
will never have any psychic experiences, because these
are as natural as breathing. It does mean that he may
refuse to recognize them, and it certainly means that he
will not be able to develop psychic abilities to the
point where he has full command of them. A lack of sufficient *mana* is the primary cause of an inability to
use one's psychic potential. Fear of this potential, regardless of how much *mana* is generated, is the secondary
cause. Lack of understanding of how to apply it is the last
and most easily overcome cause.

So far we have been dealing with the negative side
of self-knowledge. Complexes are obstacles that block
the door to power, and unless we know what obstacles we
face, we are like a blind man stumbling in the dark
in an unfamiliar room filled with awkward furniture. It is
*possible* to find our way through by trial and error,
but how much easier and faster if we have our sight and
the light is on. Even better is getting free of the obstacles
by clearing them out of the way and learning how to
stay free.

### PSYCHOANALYSIS

One of the best-known systems for trying to eliminate
complexes is psychoanalysis. In simplified terms, this
consists of having a person recall incidents from the past
which may have led up to the present complex. The
theory is that mere recall and understanding of the cause
will act as a release. While there is some sound reasoning behind it, psychoanalysis is far too prolonged and
expensive to be of much use to the average person,
and in spite of efforts to make it more popular and acceptable, it is hard to avoid the idea of being sick when the
psychoanalyst keeps calling you a patient. Also, many
times the recall and conscious understanding produce no
change at all in attitudes and actions because the *ku* has

not been taught another way to be. If a person uses the realization to actually change his behavior patterns, the process has been successful. But if the person expects change to happen spontaneously, the process will fail. Amazingly, most psychoanalysts don't seem to understand this.

### MASSAGE

Rather new in the Western world, though ancient in other areas, is a system of deep massage intended to release the chronic muscle spasms that are associated with fixed complexes. This also acts to release the bound-up emotional energy which holds the complex together. As the deep-seated, hidden, and repressed emotions are released, the complex is dissipated (but not the specific memories and ideas that composed it). The best-known systems of this type are Bioenergetics and Rolfing. Both can be very effective and are much faster at releasing complexes than psychoanalysis, but they share the weakness of not taking into account the nature of the *ku*. All the energy holding the complex together can be discharged, and the person may feel completely cured at the end of the last session. But unless new behavior patterns are instituted, there is nothing to prevent the *ku* from starting right away to build up the complex again.

These systems, and various psychotherapeutic systems which advocate the discharge of emotions as a clearing method, share the idea that people are walking around filled with certain quantities of repressed emotional energy, and that once all that energy is discharged the person will be fine. Unfortunately, it doesn't work that way. Many people do walk around with a lot of energy locked up in muscle tension, but emotions are always created in the present moment by thoughts and actions which, in a sense, "feed" the complex and keep it alive. Emotional/ energy discharge can be beneficial, but it does not,

91

by itself, get rid of our deep-seated complexes.

## KAHUNA METHODS: RELEASE

The first Huna way to release complexes to be discussed is *kala*. Its outer meanings are "to loosen, untie, release, undo, forgive, pardon; to proclaim, announce; to free one from any evil influence." In code it has the meaning of "to clean the weeds out of the path of life," with weeds being one Huna symbol for fixed complexes. *Kala* includes many techniques that Westerners would find unrelated. That is because the kahunas look at things in terms of energy flow, and as far as they are concerned an idea or belief can block energy flow as much as muscle tension can. So part of *kala* is the practice of *lomi-lomi*, probably best described as "bioenergetic massage." Even that is inadequate, however, because in true *lomi-lomi* the practitioner is also working on the mind of the recipient. *Lomi-lomi*, then, is like a combination of Swedish or Esalen massage, acupressure, polarity therapy, and positive mental programming. The body and energy work helps to release the blockages, while at the same time the mental work gives the energy new direction and sets new patterns.

*Kala* is also the technique of forgiveness, both of yourself and of others. It is amazing how much energy people lock up and waste in guilt and resentment, energy that could be used to heal and create. As a technique, forgiveness includes confession—an open acknowledgement, even to yourself, of what has been done wrong—repentance, and absolution. In the Catholic Church this has been formalized into an institutional ritual, but the same process occurs in informal forgiveness.

Confession itself helps to start the flow of painfully blocked energy of the complex, and it really doesn't matter to whom or what you confess. Many people get great relief from telling their guilts and resentments to a friend, a psychotherapist, a minister, or even a tree.

Writing them out to yourself may also produce a surprising amount of release. The point is to bring the situation into full conscious awareness.

Repentance, which may include atonement, has been greatly misunderstood. It is almost always interpreted as meaning "to feel sorry or miserable about what you have done." That doesn't do you or anyone else any good. What repentance really means is to change your way of thinking and to act differently. Just to feel sorry is meaningless; you have to do something about it. That something may be an attitude you can change or an act you can perform quite on your own, or it may have to involve someone else, in which case it is called "atonement."

Now atonement is another word that has been greatly misunderstood. It is usually taken to mean that you have to "pay back" a person or society or even God for something you did wrong, and this paying back can be in the form of money, a good deed, or the undergoing of punishment. All of this is a distortion. Atonement actually means "to become reconciled" (i.e., "friendly again," from the Middle English *at one*, "in accord") or "to make amends." The latter term, "amends," means "to improve one's conduct," not to make up for something or to pay for something (cf. Webster's *New World Dictionary*).

The third step in forgiveness, absolution (the same thing as pardon) comes from a Latin word meaning "to set free," and is essentially a declaration that one is free from guilt, blame, or obligation.

In practical terms to forgive yourself, you acknowledge your mistake, change your ways, and make the decision to pardon yourself. Of course, it is nice if someone else pardons you, but that won't have any effect unless you accept it, so it all comes down to pardoning yourself. If feeling guilty is habitual, even if you have changed your ways, then you will have to replace it with the habit of feeling pardoned. If you have the belief that you

93

should be punished, then you must either eliminate the "should" idea from your consciousness or find a way to punish yourself *once* that will be effective in convincing your *ku* that it's enough, while not being too harmful.

To forgive someone else, first acknowledge his mistake in your own mind (it really doesn't matter if the other person acknowledges it; it's your complex you are working with), change how you think about and behave toward the person you've been resenting, and make the decision to pardon him. Some ways to change your thinking are to change your expectations (I often have people forgive others for being imperfect), increase your tolerance, and/or reduce or eliminate your "shoulds" in regard to other people's behavior. Something I have found to be very effective is to mentally give the other person permission to have done what he did, or to be the way he is. This doesn't mean that it is good or that you like it. But giving permission for the behavior to have happened or to exist now helps to free you from its effect. I don't claim that getting rid of resentment is easy, but if it is interfering with your health, happiness, or success, the effort is worth it.

### HYPNOSIS

Another kahuna method for opening the door to power and getting free is hypnosis, including self-hypnosis. The Hawaiian word I use for this is *kupono*. Hypnosis is essentially a process whereby the subconscious is convinced that something is true. When this becomes a habitual belief, then it automatically manifests in thought and behavior. In terms of complexes, this procedure is especially good for getting rid of fears and establishing confidence. There are a multitude of books that describe a multitude of hypnotic techniques, but the absolutely essential ingredient for successful hypnosis is continued or repetitive concentration on an idea in such a way that you create a habitual response to the idea. If you are anxious about money, for instance, you can use hypnosis to replace that fear with confident attitudes, feelings, and behaviors regarding money. If you are afraid of meeting people, hypnosis can help you become a confident conversationalist or speaker.

The main tools of hypnosis are words, images, and feelings. The words (descriptions, affirmations, commands, and/or directions) and the images (multisensory imagination is best) are used to create positive emotional/physical feelings related to the desired aim. This can produce virtually instantaneous results where there are no blocking complexes, but if there are it can take any length of time from a few minutes to a number of months, depending on the nature of the complex and the intensity and consistency of your motivation to change.

Following is a simple kind of self-hypnotic programming that you can use to good effect in getting rid of complexes:

1. Acknowledge the condition you want to change.

2. Define its positive opposite (e.g., fear into confidence, poverty into abundance, etc.).

3. Imagine yourself in the new condition, or write out a description of it.

4. Repeatedly bring this image or description to mind, and forcefully tell/remind yourself that "You can do it . . . do it!" When you get a positive feeling from this, you will know that you are reaching the subconscious. When the new condition is habitual in your life, you will know your subconscious has accepted it completely.

Repeat this process until you have the results you want. In this form of self-hypnosis, you do not have to close your eyes or relax or do anything out of the ordinary unless you want to. Naturally, a good hypnotherapist whom you trust can be of immense help, but you can do it on your

own by using one of the good books on self-hypnosis
that are available, and by applying a great deal of self-
discipline.

### ACTIVATING POWER

A third kahuna method is given the generic name of
*hana mana*, "activating power," which refers to a variety
of techniques for increasing personal power. The
idea behind this is that all complexes are based on a
fundamental premise of helplessness or insecurity, and
they can be removed by the development of true
power or strength. I say "true" because complexes themselves are attempts to cope with insecurity by using
manipulation instead of power and rigidity, instead of
strength, neither of which is satisfying or very effective.

A person with true power or *mana* that is highly
developed steps right out of the "fight or flight" way of
coping with problems and operates from a position
of deep inner strength. At this level he is consciously in
touch with motivations and objectives and thinks and
acts appropriately rather than by reflex. Such a level, possible for every human being, is reached by developing
powers or strengths as follows:

> *Mental strength*, by practicing directed thought, i.e.,
> choosing the quality and nature of your thinking,
> including your imagination, and by consciously deny-
> ing, refuting, canceling or eliminating (not repressing)
> any kinds of thoughts that you decide are not good
> for you.

> *Physical strength*, by practicing directed function.
> In other words, by consciously telling your body what to
> do, how to act, and how to feel. This includes direct-
> ing the various parts or systems of your body as well.
> Physical strength, in this sense, is not limited to muscular
> power. It includes feelings because these are sensed
> through the body.

> *Spiritual strength*, by practicing directed life force
> or *mana*. This means becoming more and more aware of

*mana* as it flows in and around you, and it means learning how to direct its flow, intensity, and effect by words, images, and will.

As your mind, body, and spirit grow stronger under your conscious direction, old complexes based on fear and doubt will dissolve and fade away. I cannot go into a great deal of detail on the *hana mana* method, but here is a simple guideline that will take you a long way. They translate the powers to be developed into practical effects.

For your mind, cultivate a positive attitude toward everyone and everything. This doesn't mean to pretend that everything is fine. It means to look for the good in everything, and if you can't find any, figure out a way to put some in.

For your body, cultivate a positive self-image, including appearance, activity, and emotional state, and coach yourself into making the ideal real.

For your spirit, cultivate the habit of deep breathing and learn something about the art of bioenergetic healing and meditation.

### ELIMINATING COMPLEXES

A fixed complex is like a stronger than normal habit. Any habit can be replaced by another habit, but some habits are easier to replace then others, depending on the motivations for their existence. The following comments apply to all habitual behavior, whether mental, emotional, or physical.

Let's use a cigarette habit as an example. The process of change when this is an ordinary habit goes like this: The smoker decides to quit, experiences a slight increase in the urge to smoke, refuses to give in to it, and the urge and habit fade away. An estimated 80% of all smokers who quit simply do so on their own with very little trouble.

If cigarette smoking is a manifestation of a complex,

however, it usually goes like this: The smoker decides to quit, experiences a strong increase in the urge to smoke, refuses to give in. The urge gets stronger and stronger. The person feels helpless and gives in to the urge rather than go crazy.

The key word above is "helpless." The purpose of any habit arising out of a complex is to enable a person to cope with situations that make him feel helpless or inadequate. If the coping habit is beneficial and doesn't interfere with the person's growth and happiness, then there's no particular reason to change it. But if not, then the most successful results are obtained by increasing the person's overall sense of strength, power, and competence. As the level of personal power increases, both the coping habit and its complex source lose their reason for existence. When that happens, they disappear because the subconscious does not maintain any habits or complexes that do not serve a purpose.

In getting rid of a complex and its habits (often called compulsions or obsessions), be prepared for a magnification of the urge to return to or continue the habit behavior. This magnification is temporary, but it may seem irresistible at the time. Refuse to give in anyway, to the extent that you can, and use all the Huna methods as appropriate to help you free yourself from your blocks. The thing to remember is that any idea or feeling which is acted upon is reinforced, and any idea or feeling that you refrain from acting upon is weakened.

# 9

# The Road to Self-Mastery

Mastery of your "hidden self" refers to the establish-
ment of a directing relationship with your subconscious
mind. You can learn to control your subconscious, but
not in the sense of a master-slave relationship, because that simply doesn't work for very long. Rigid,
authoritarian control over your subconscious is what
leads to physical, emotional, mental, and spiritual break-
downs. On the other hand, giving up conscious control
will result in your being controlled by your subconscious
and all the various influences that it is subject to. Self-
improvement is impossible under such circumstances.
What you want to develop is firm guidance, by your
conscious mind. It is vital, if you want to accomplish anything in Huna, for your conscious mind to undertake
its primary responsibility as teacher and guide to the
subconscious.

EMOTIONAL FREEDOM

One of the curious teachings of Huna is that you must
separate in order to unite. What this means is that in

99

order to master your subconscious you must become more aware of it through a process of disidentification. Only then can you consciously integrate your *ku* and guide it. It is like learning a physical skill, such as a martial art. You can go ahead and learn just the moves and do fairly well. But if you want to become a true expert, you must separate your mind from your body to study the latter's anatomy and physiology. With that awareness you can reintegrate your mind and body and move with more precision and control.

The important concept is that of ceasing to identify with the emotional reactions of your subconscious. When you say "I am angry," you are identifying with the subconscious, and you may find it extremely difficult to get rid of the anger. The fact of the matter is that you are consciously aware of anger; you are feeling or experiencing anger. From this "witnessing" position you can view the emotion more objectively and have more capacity to change it. The conscious mind by itself is unemotional. When an emotional response causes you to engage in a physical action "without thinking," it is because the conscious has allowed the subconscious to take over. By learning to immediately take an objective viewpoint when emotions surface, you can control their direction or even sap them of their strength.

Emotions can arise from innumerable causes. Some have a reasonable basis and some appear to be completely illogical. One technique of control is to analyze the purpose and origin of the emotion as soon as it starts. You can ask yourself questions like: Where did this emotion come from? Why am I feeling it now? Is it appropriate to this situation? Does it seem reasonable? Should it be changed? What makes my subconscious feel this way? If the purpose and origin of the emotion cannot be found right away, it does not matter too much at this point. It is more important for now to learn to dissociate your conscious mind from the response and refuse to let it sweep you along with it. If you are persistent enough, you will soon find that the analysis itself tends to drain the emotion of its power, because you are diverting the energy of the emotion to the conscious thinking process.

Where the emotion remains strong, you have the conscious choice and ability to redirect it. Anger may make you want to strike out at someone, but you can hit a pillow just as well. Your subconscious might not find that quite as satisfying, but the effect will be almost the same—and far safer, as the pillow cannot strike back. If you feel like screaming with frustration, don't hold back. Walk into the bathroom, put your face in a towel, and scream your heart out. The energy of the emotion will be discharged in a harmless way, and you will feel much better for it. Engaging in physical labor or exercise are well-known methods for working off negative emotions, also. From the Huna point of view, though, maintaining an objective awareness of the emotion is just as important as discharging or redirecting the energy.

One thing to avoid as much as possible is attempting to suppress the emotion, which actually means clamping down on your muscles to keep from feeling the emotion. Many people have learned how to do this so well that they don't even know it is happening; their subconscious does it out of habit. The more emotions you lock away from your awareness like this, the more you will be subject to physical ailments, messy relationships, subconscious control, and control by others. Much of the problem of suppressed emotions comes from a false assumption, held by many people, that if you feel an emotion you must act on it. This is simply not true. It is entirely possible to feel an emotion very strongly and just not do anything but feel it. The kahuna technique for this is to learn how to relax your muscles at will. It is a physiological fact that you can't carry out any physical action if your muscles are completely relaxed. It is also a fact that if your muscles are completely relaxed, you can't even *experience* a strong emotion. So, in order to feel an emotion without taking any action, relax your muscles just enough to keep you from moving (don't *tense* them, *relax* them!). In order to keep from experiencing a strong emotion, learn to relax your muscles completely.

Of course it is negative emotion that you want most to control. But it is good to experience the objectivity of the positive emotions, too, if only to realize that they also originate with the subconscious and not the conscious. You need not turn yourself into a cold-blooded machine. But even positive emotions can have negative results, and emotions should always work for you and not against you. By developing the ability to "stand apart" when emotions sweep over you, you will be taking a giant step toward self-mastery.

### EXTENDING AWARENESS

Learning to control the subconscious is intimately connected to learning how to listen to it. The subconscious is bombarded with a vast amount of sensory input every moment of the day, but most of this is ignored by the conscious mind. In a sense this is necessary if we are not to be eternally distracted, but in another sense we are missing quite a lot out of life. To give an example, suppose you are discussing an important project with a friend or business associate. You can see the expression on his face, hear his words, perhaps touch his hand or arm. Normally this would be all you would pay attention to. But your subconscious also notices the way he is sitting, the positioning of his arms and legs, the changes in his skin tone, the quality of his voice, the movement of his eyes, and the "atmosphere" around him, all of which can tell how he really feels about the subject of your discussion. This is information which you can become consciously aware of, learn to interpret, and utilize in your daily living. Keep in mind, however, that whatever is going on with another person is a statement about that person, not about you.

If other people are constantly giving off signals about themselves, then so are you, both externally and internally. The more you become aware of your own signals, the more you can direct them in ways of your own choosing. For instance, pay attention to your body the next time you are with a group of people. In all likelihood, if you are really being aware, you will notice that small areas of muscles tend to tighten up when certain people are near or when certain topics are spoken of. This will usually occur in the hips, legs, and/or shoulders. After becoming aware of it, you can consciously relax these areas, paying attention as well to any feelings that may arise as you do so. These tensions and feelings will give you more information about your subconscious reactions in certain situations, and through awareness you can give direction in a positive way.

In a similar fashion, you can learn to be aware of subconscious thoughts or images that cross your mind in certain situations or with certain people. When these are of an unpleasant or unwanted nature, most people try to force them out or suppress them, as they do with emotions. Much more effective is a process of "relaxing" the mind. To do this, you focus your attention externally. For example, you can look at something in your environment and be aware of its color, shape, and texture and nothing else; you can listen to something and be aware of its tone, pitch, and loudness; or you can touch something and be aware of its density, shape, and texture. Doing any of these things is like relaxing your mental muscles, so that you can then redirect your thoughts in a conscious way. It is also a good way to become more aware of your outer environment.

### REPROGRAMMING

Your subconscious, like any creature of habit, will go on doing a thing in a certain way until you take time to teach it otherwise, or until it learns from someone else without your knowledge. Some people have experienced this while driving a car. When they first learn to drive, they have to concentrate very hard on each movement. After a while, they can leave most of the driving to the subconscious while they talk, listen to the radio, or look at the scenery. But if they should change cars, especially from a stick shift to an automatic, they find that the habit pattern gets them into trouble, and the subconscious has to be taught a new way of driving. Just as you get into patterns of physical action, so do you get into patterns of thought. Habitual thinking patterns are even harder to change than physical habits, but it certainly can be done. For most of us it *must* be done if we are to progress and grow.

The conscious mind has the responsibility for programming, or setting the pattern, for the thought reactions of the subconscious mind. If you want to change the habitual thinking of the subconscious, you must consciously keep the desired pattern in the forefront of your mind until the subconscious has accepted it as a new habit. This is the method behind the success of "positive thinking," affirmations, and hypnotic therapy. The subconscious is very susceptible to repeated suggestion, but if the reprogramming is not complete, the subconscious will revert to its old habits once the repetition has ceased. Lack of perseverance is the reason for the many failures. Using suggestion is not like waving a magic wand. You don't do it for a certain number of times, or for a certain period of time, and then just lay back and watch it work. Using suggestion is more like using a shovel. You just keep using it until the job is done and you have the results you want. Basically, you keep on suggesting or affirming until your subconscious is convinced that what you are saying is true.

104

Only then will a new habit be established. Depending on your existing degree of fear, doubt, or contrary ideas, you may need only one suggestion or affirmation to make a change, or you may need a million. At any rate, the secret is not to give up until you get results.

What kind of results? Hate can be changed to love; insecurity and inferiority to confidence; frustration to calm acceptance; a sense of purposelessness to powerful ambition. There is hardly any limit to how much we can change ourselves and, consequently, change the way people react toward us. All it takes is a goal, desire, and stamina. For a lot of people this seems like too much, but if you refuse to take advantage of the tools that are available for building a better life, you have only yourself to blame.

### INCREASING POWER

One of the functions of your subconscious is to serve as a power or energy distributor. It is not your source of power—that is a function of your High Self—but by the nature of its habits it does determine how much power or energy you have available at any given time. Your potential energy is infinite; your effective energy is limited by your subconscious beliefs and habits. To increase your effective energy and power, you will have to find some way of changing or overcoming any limitations you may have established.

Everything in this world is accomplished by the transformation of one kind of energy into another. This is as true for the personal circumstances of your life as it is for the changing of water into steam or gasoline into motive force in a car. The amount of energy or *mana* flowing in your system will determine your state of health, your confidence, your effect on others, and the achievement of your goals. If you only have a small amount of personal energy flow, you will only have small effects in your life, even though your subconscious may have accepted all your suggestions and affirmations.

The more energy you have, the greater the effects you can produce. A strong build-up of personal energy can even wipe away doubts and fears without a lot of suggestion or affirmation. Just think of how confident you feel when you are also feeling very healthy. Health is nothing more than a high energy state; the more energy you have flowing, the healthier you are.

Now it is important not to confuse flowing energy with tension energy. When you are filled with flowing energy, you feel healthy, happy, confident, strong, relaxed, and energized all at the same time, and you don't feel wiped out after any kind of work. When you are filled with tension energy, you feel nervous, irritable, uptight, upset, edgy, and you feel wiped out after almost any kind of effort. The difference is that flowing energy draws upon the unlimited energy of the universe, and tension energy only draws upon whatever energy resources you happen to have in your body at the time. It is like the difference in producing a stronger spurt of water from a hose by opening the valve wider at the source or by just squeezing the hose.

How do you tap into universal energy? Not by consciously willing it. You have to master the processes which will induce the subconscious to let the energy in and allow it to increase. These processes can be divided into three categories: visual, auditory, and kinesthetic. Below are some potent examples of each:

### Visual

Imagine that you are taking a shower in a waterfall of pure, tingling energy that soaks into every cell of your body.

Imagine that there are lines of light connecting you to all the stars and galaxies. Then imagine that on your command all that energy comes from them to you in waves of light.

## Auditory

Repeated suggestion that you are being filled with unlimited universal energy.

Chant a power phrase like *OM* or *aumakua kia manawa.*

Listen *completely* to powerful music.

## Kinesthetic

Breathe very slowly and deeply, until you feel highly energized.

Do some vigorous exercise or movements *and* get very emotionally excited in a positive way.

## Combination

Imagine that you are achieving something that you want very much; affirm that you have unlimited power and energy to do it; get emotionally enthusiastic about doing it and about the benefits of doing it; consciously and strongly *intend* that it shall be done.

The latter, of course, is a way of mobilizing and motivating your subconscious to work toward the particular goal you have in mind, and of providing the energy for its manifestation.

### TALK TO YOURSELF

Your subconscious is always listening to your speech, watching your imagery, and feeling your attitudes. It is also always presenting ideas, images, and feelings for your conscious decision as to what to do with them. Often these impressions are stimulated by outside events and are not necessarily part of your ordinary or even habitual thinking. Whatever your conscious reaction to these presentations is, your subconscious takes that as a direct order. Except for instinctual drives and processes like hunger and digestion, your subconscious contains nothing but what you have consciously put in it, allowed in it, or paid no attention to. Nevertheless, it will constantly bring things to your awareness so you can pass judgment on them, whether you know what is happening or not.

The subconscious needs and craves direction. If it doesn't get it from you, it will take it from the world: your parents, your teachers, your friends and colleagues, your religious or governmental leaders. How many ideas that you express are really yours, and how many did you pick up from someone else without thinking them through? Listen to yourself speak sometime and you may be surprised at how many other people are speaking through your mouth. If you don't direct your subconscious, someone else will.

The ultimate in mastery of your hidden self is to take conscious direction over everything your subconscious does and conscious responsibility for it. This doesn't mean that you try to control what it does— you don't take charge of your heartbeat or your walking, for instance. But you do tell your subconscious what to do, even if it is already being done, in order to make it even better.

A simple and highly effective technique is to start out each day by talking to your subconscious as if you were talking to someone ready and willing to carry out your orders, directives, or instructions. In actuality, you may get cheerful willingness on some things, stalling on others, and outright resistance on still others. But you must keep giving the directions that you want carried out until you get results. In some ways the subconscious is like a bureaucracy that has gotten used to a particular routine which may or may not be efficient and effective. Following this analogy, you as a conscious mind are like a newly appointed director of this bureaucracy, intent on changing old policies and procedures. You will get cooperation in areas where the benefits to the "employees" are obvious, and resistance where benefits are not so obvious or do not seem better than old ways of doing things. Even the cooperation will last only if the bureaucracy is convinced that you are sincere and if you continue the new policies until they become routine.

To carry out this directive role, I suggest that you use an idea developed by Dr. Frederick Eikerenkoetter. Instead of speaking to your subconscious as a single entity, speak to your thoughts, your feelings, and your body in some way like the following:

"Thoughts, listen up! I want you to stop being so scattered and to stop wasting your time and energy with fears and doubts and worries and old memories that don't do us any good. From now on I want you to think only good thoughts, positive thoughts, and loving thoughts. Think about beautiful things, about our goals and plans, about ways of helping others, and ways of improving ourself. Thoughts, think only good thoughts. If any other kinds come up, look at them, kick them out, and go back to good thoughts.

"Feelings, listen up! I want you to stop dwelling on fears and anxieties, old hurts and grudges, anger, resentment, guilt, jealousy, and any of those things. If any of those come up, go ahead and feel them for a little bit, and then let them fade away and replace them with good feelings. I want you to dwell on good feelings, happy feelings, confident feelings, successful feelings, and loving feelings. I want you to have these kinds of feelings all the time, from now on.

"Body, listen up! You're a great body, and you do all kinds of wonderful things like pumping blood and replacing cells that I don't even have to tell you to do. But now I want you to do everything even better. I want you to increase our energy, strength, and health in all ways, to be more skillful and graceful in all you do, to utilize food and air even more efficiently than you already do, and to stop doing anything which takes away our strength, energy, and health. And body, I want you to relax more, feel pleasure more, enjoy life more, and give more pleasure to others.

"Thank you Thoughts, thank you Feelings, thank you Body, thank you God-in-me!"

Naturally, you may modify this "script" to suit your own purposes, but it can lead you to greater mastery of your hidden self.

# 10

## Your Superconscious Self

The superconscious or High Self of Huna is called *aumakua* in Hawaiian. In the dictionary it is defined as "a personal god" and as a figurative expression for "a trustworthy person." As used in Huna, it is "God within you." Since the code language of Hawaiian is the key to all our understanding of Huna, we can do no better than to start by exploring the hidden meanings of *aumakua* in order to reveal the deeper implications of the Huna definition.

### THE PARENTAL SELF

*Au*, the first syllable, has "self" as one of its meanings, and *makua* means "parent" (either father or mother). A simple translation, then, is "parent-self." Some of the early missionaries to Hawaii thought this was a reference to ancestor worship, but to the kahunas it would be more accurately described as "source self," for they were well aware that our origin is in spirit and that our physical parents and ancestors are channels for, not

111

creators of, our being. How well this was recognized is shown by the fact that the word for ancestor was *kupuna*, which can be translated as "source of the subconscious," a reference to the beliefs, attitudes, and physical heredity carried on through subconscious memory from generation to generation.

*Au makua* means "your father" and *a'u makua* means "my father." Bear this in mind for I will point out its significance later on. *Au* also means "older," which emphasizes the parental aspect and indicates that the High Self is more highly evolved than the physical personality.

The same word also means "current," as in a stream, a reference to the flow of *mana* between the conscious, subconscious, and superconscious selves, and "movement of thought," showing the guidance we receive from the superconscious through thoughts and ideas that rise in the mind.

Other meanings involving swimming and dousing reveal the High Self giving us *mana* and teaching us how to live. *Makua* was later used with true understanding to indicate "the Lord God" of the Christians. From these meanings we get a good picture of a highly evolved, supportive and guardian spirit, an ideal parent.

### THE MANIFESTING SPIRIT

The root *ma* has a translation of "by means of." As part of the word *aumakua*, it refers to the role of the High Self in making things happen. When added to the root *kua*, the reference is even clearer, because this means to carve things out of wood, to make tapa cloth, or to form things on an anvil. These are analogies for producing physical experience out of nonphysical thought and *aka* or etheric matter. This meaning is emphasized further by the root *maku*, which means "to harden, gel, solidify."

In Huna, the visible, physical matter and circumstances of this world are believed to exist first as thought forms or, to use the convenient expression of Edward R. Russell, "T-fields" of *aka* matter, charged with the minimum amount of *mana* required to hold them together in a specified pattern. In order for anything to exist as a visible, tangible, or measurable reality, it must be brought "down" from the world of form into our three-dimensional world. This can only be accomplished if the *aka* T-field receives a sufficient amount of *mana* to allow it to manifest. Our whole physical universe was apparently created first as an immense T-field of an Ultimate Being and brought into manifestation by being charged through and through with *mana*, the universal prime energy.

On a far more local level, we as human beings constantly surround ourselves with T-fields or thought patterns of our own making. As we continue to pour *mana* into them by thinking the same thoughts over the years, the patterns become so habitual and strengthened that we no longer think of them consciously. Yet they form the patterns for the manifesting of our daily lives.

The manifesting of personal reality requires cooperation by the three selves of an individual, though obviously the conscious mind may not be aware of what is going on. To gain a better understanding of the process, let's describe it as a series of steps:

1. The conscious mind focuses attention on something (a thought, object or event).

2. The subconscious mind treats the focus of attention as an event and retains a memory of it.

3. The superconscious mind uses the memory as a pattern or blueprint to create an equivalent physical experience.

The above is an *extremely* simplified but substantially correct explanation of the process of manifestation. Where there are no conflicting beliefs or doubts, the mere focus of attention will stir the superconscious into action. Suppose you hear an unusual name, for instance, and you let your mind dwell on it for a few moments. As long as the channels are clear, the likelihood is that the name will pop up in various ways in your life for awhile without any further effort on your part. If the conscious mind focuses on something and decides that it is true or a fact of life, then the subconscious will maintain that as a belief or habitual attitude, and the superconscious will make it a more or less permanent part of your life.

The superconscious manifests your physical experience by using the patterns of your conscious and subconscious thoughts. It does not need *mana* or energy from these two selves to do its work because it is directly in touch with infinite energy. The idea that you must send *mana* to the High Self before it can operate in the physical world is incorrect and has caused a great deal of confusion among Huna students. The fact that manifestation occurs constantly in your life without any effort or energy build-up is clear proof that the superconscious has access to plenty of energy to work with. And yet, the conscious build-up of *mana*, especially emotional *mana*, often does seem to produce better results. Why is that?

The fact is that building up your *mana* through desire, enthusiasm, excitement, deep breathing, visualization, etc. can serve an important purpose, that of overriding existing beliefs and doubts that are interfering with the manifestation you desire. In other words, it is your subconscious that needs the extra *mana*, not your superconscious. Beliefs are energy-charged ideas that form a strong pattern, and some have a higher charge than others. You could say that in a way some of them are "louder" than others and therefore easier for the superconscious to hear. In order to change an existing condition, you either have to turn off the beliefs that are forming the pattern for the experience or you have to make some new or more positive beliefs "loud" enough to drown the others out. Consciously increasing your personal *mana* while keeping your aim in mind is one way of drowning out old fears and doubts.

In very basic terms, then, manifestation follows attention. The more attention you give to something, consciously or subconsciously, the more it manifests in your life. The more "pure" the attention, the clearer the results, and the more scattered the attention, the more mixed the results. Conscious attention is a matter of choice; subconscious attention is a matter of habit. The superconscious will always manifest what you focus on, whether it is pleasant or unpleasant, but it will always inspire you in some way toward a better focus if you are willing to listen.

## THE DIVINE SPIRIT

Investigating further the code meanings of *aumakua*, we find that *akua* is defined in the Hawaiian dictionary as a god, a spirit, or something divine. This concept of an inner god is directly related to Jesus' depiction of the Father in the New Testament, yet the relationship is so intimate, so misunderstood, that it has escaped all but a very few. A code translation of the Gospels shows very clearly that Jesus understood God the Father to be none other than the superconscious recognized by Huna. At the beginning of this discussion I stressed the code meanings of "your father" and "my father." Read the New Testament carefully and you will see that Jesus, in all but a single instance, speaks of "My Father" or "Your Father." "Let your light shine before men, in order that they may see your good works and give glory to your Father in heaven" (Matt. 5:16). "You therefore are to be perfect, even as your heavenly Father is perfect" (Matt. 5:48). "All things have been delivered to me by my Father" (Luke 10:22). "And I appoint to you a kingdom, even as my Father has appointed to me" (Luke 22:29). The use of "my" and "your" is a clear outer indication that Jesus meant the High Self of the individual.

This is made even more clear when we take the single instance when Jesus is recorded to have said "Our Father." This occurs in Matthew 6:9 when Jesus is giving the formula for a proper prayer action. The phrase in Hawaiian is *E ko makou Makua.* Hawaiian has sixteen different forms of the word *our* so when this phrase was chosen to translate the English words by the kahunas who helped the early missionaries, there had to be a very specific understanding of what was meant. This particular form means a single object possessed individually by several people. In English it would be like a speaker saying to a crowd of unrelated people, "We should all honor our father on Father's Day." Jesus, then, was referring to each individual's superconscious. It is worth noting, however, that Luke (11:12) leaves out the "Our" entirely.

A very brief glance at Buddhism and yoga will show that they also contain the Huna concept of an individual, personalized "god-self." Buddhists bow, not to each other, but to the "Buddha-self" of the other person. Some yogis respect, revere, and pray to the Mother, which is only another term for the female aspect of the *aumakua.*

What about God the Absolute, the Ultimate Being? Such a one must certainly exist, or this ordered universe would not exist, but this must not be confused with the personal superconscious. It is an arrogant and incredible assumption that man as we know and see him is the last word in evolution. To postulate a great leap from imperfect man to Ultimate Perfection is to postulate the absurd. On purely logical grounds, it stands to reason that there must be something in between. It seems almost impious to believe that Ultimate God could do no better than man before arriving back at Divine Being.

Of course, nearly all religions speak of superior beings called angels, but they have been out of fashion for some time now. Huna suggests that the concept be brought back into awareness. In many ways the superconscious is like a guardian angel, always looking out for our highest good, always giving us advice on how to improve ourselves, always ready to lend a helping hand when we ask in the right way.

That right way has nothing to do with pleading or begging or beseeching or crying for help. It is concerned with giving clear statements and directions. In the Psalms and in the Gospels (the 23rd Psalm and the Lord's Prayer, for instance) the speakers make statements of fact and give clear directions for action. Simply put, that right way has to do with telling your High Self what to do by means of words, images, and feelings, giving thanks that it is being done, and refusing to entertain any thoughts of fear and doubt. The superconscious, your personal god within, will be even more active in your life when you acknowledge and communicate in this way.

This concept of a very personal God does not in any way negate the usefulness of praying to Jesus, the Buddha, the saints, or any other gods or goddesses of a particular religion. It only implies that no matter to whom you address your prayers, they first pass through your own *aumakua*. Since your superconscious is part and parcel of your own nature, it is still *you* reaching out to whatever higher entities you want to contact. If your High Self does need help in its endeavors, trust it to make the right contact in the right way.

Consider the possibility, then, and accept as a hypothesis for the time being, that you have a High Self who is your constant guide and companion, not only ready but anxious to help you on your way toward perfection. Your *aumakua* can help you rid yourself of all the unnecessary negative conditions of your life and help you to understand and benefit from those which seem negative but are necessary. You are never alone. Huna shows that God is far more personal than most

117

people would have ever thought possible.

### THE COMPANY OF HIGH SELVES

Everyone and everything has an *aumakua*. Any interacting group of beings or things has its own group spirit, what the kahunas would call the Company of High Selves (*poe aumakua*). This group spirit is not just individual High Selves grouped together, but a whole entity in its own right, just as you are a whole person even though you are composed physically of billions of individual cells. Whenever there is a group or area identity, then, there is a High Self of that group, which is a fuller expression of the individual High Selves that form it.

For example, the human race has an *aumakua*, of which you are a part, and the same is true for your nation, your state, your community, and your family, as well as for your clubs, your church, your committees, your work team, and any other group to which you belong. And just as you can contact your own High Self for aid and guidance, so you can contact the *aumakua* of any of your groups for the same purpose.

### CONTACTING THE HIGH SELF

Your *aumakua* operates in your life whether you are aware of it or not. However, the more aware of it you are, the more abundantly and fruitfully it can help you. Conscious contact leads to more effective manifestation of whatever it is you want in life. Here are a number of ways to make that contact.

1. *Inward Quest.* This is not an easy way, but it has been used by many saints and sages all over the world. Here I will give you one simple variation. Sit by yourself with your eyes open or closed and ask yourself questions like these: Who is aware of sitting here? Who is aware of this body, these feelings, these thoughts? Who is aware of being aware? Keep asking such questions

about every sensation, feeling, or thought that comes into your awareness, *without demanding, making up, expecting, or looking for any answers.* After a time (sorry, I can't be more specific), you will break through into a greater awareness, which is the direct contact with your High Self.

2. *Praise the Present.* This one is suitable for everybody. All it takes is paying attention to all the beauty and goodness in your immediate environment and complimenting or praising whomever and whatever you can. You have to really focus on the present moment and avoid any analysis or criticism. When you are successful, you will feel a growing sense of expansion and good feeling, which is your contact with your High Self. This one usually doesn't take long at all.

3. *Energy Awareness.* In a sense your *aumakua* can be thought of as pure, conscious energy. The kahunas would symbolize this as light, as a flowing current in the body, as a beautiful sound (including music), as a delicious taste, and as a delightful perfume, depending on individual preference and sensitivity. Most usual is the combination of imagining yourself surrounded by light while feeling a flow of energy through your body. With practice this becomes awareness, not just imagination, and is your sign of High Self contact.

4. *Meeting the Wise One.* This starts out as a mental adventure and gradually turns into a sure form of contact with your *aumakua.* In one simple version you imagine yourself going along a path until you find a very wise man, woman, or couple. Any of these symbolize your High Self. Then you sit with these wise ones, talk with them, touch them, and listen to what they have to tell you as guidance for your life. Know beforehand that what you will get is advice; any decision-making will be left up to you. If you seem to get orders, some part of your subconscious is distorting the contact.

119

5. *Expanding Identity.* This requires a particular ability to extend your sense of identity into your environment until you can feel that the people and things around you are no more separate from you than are your own hands and feet. The degree of oneness that you experience is a measure of contact with your *aumakua*.

Once contact is made by any method, you can enjoy it for its own refreshing sake, or proceed to focus on what you would like your *aumakua* to manifest. Frequent contact with your superconscious is an important way of mastering yourself and your life.

# 11

## Dream Talk

A Chinese philosopher once dreamed that he was a butterfly dreaming that he was a man. When he woke up he was not sure whether he was still the butterfly dreaming that he was a man or a man who had dreamed that he was a butterfly.

The point of this story is that the world of dreams into which we slip off and on every night is every bit as real as this conscious, orderly one to which we are more accustomed. Most of us have been conditioned by our culture to pay very little attention to dreams, and in the process we end up ignoring at least one third of our life. For sleep is not oblivion. It is a time of learning, of play, of praise, criticism, and balancing—of communication with our Higher Self and other forces, powers, and people. It is another dimension where we are often more active than we are in this one.

If you have never explored the world of dreams, now is the time to start. You will find adventure, a great many surprises, tremendous beauty, and probably a share of ugliness and evil. You will be exploring the vast, uncharted territory of your own mind, meeting friends and enemies and yourself in many guises.

### THE DREAMING PROCESS

Every human being dreams every night. There is much evidence to indicate that animals do, too, but we are concerned now with humans. Even if you cannot recall a single dream that you have ever had, this does not mean that you do not dream. It only means you do not remember dreaming.

The fact that everyone dreams has long been known to students of the esoteric sciences, and research scientists have proven it to their satisfaction in the laboratory as well. According to these studies, we dream in cycles throughout the night, and we dream two distinct types of dreams. One is a "straight" dream that reflects activities like those in the fully waking state without distortion. The other type is longer, more vivid, and seems to break all the rules of time, space, and logic. It is precisely because of this type that dreams have so often been considered unreal and unworthy of attention.

Research shows we *have* to dream—it is vital to our physical and mental health. When people are experimentally deprived of dreaming for a certain period, they dream even more when next allowed to sleep uninterruptedly, as if to make up for what was lost. If the dreaming is interrupted for longer periods, they begin to dream on their feet, in which case the dreams are called hallucinations.

Actually, we all dream all the time. I am not speaking about the idea that this outer life is but a dream, though a very good case could be made for that. What I mean is that dreams—inner experiences both "straight" and strange—are occurring all the time just beneath our usual waking consciousness. Most people have been conditioned not to pay attention to them. But if you just sit down, close your eyes, and watch what happens, you will experience a dream of some kind, even while you are wide awake. It may happen immediately or it may take awhile, depending on your present state and previous conditioning. But dream you surely will. There is even good reason to believe that frequent recourse to "waking dreaming" will lessen the need for "sleep dreaming." Thomas Edison, for instance, used to take about seventeen very brief naps a day and only needed three hours of sleep at night. He didn't take the naps to sleep or rest but purposely to dream.

### THE HUNA VIEWPOINT

The most common word for *dream* is *moe 'uhane*, which literally means "spirit sleep." A code meaning is "the spirit breaks away and goes elsewhere." Specifically, it refers to the dreams you have during a deep, sound sleep. According to Hawaiian tradition, your spirit goes traveling, seeing persons and places, encountering other spirits, experiencing adventures, and passing on messages from your *aumakua* or High Self. All of these events you remember as dreams.

Among the many sorts of dream experiences are messages from the subconscious relating to our state of health and suggesting how to improve it. Other dreams from the same source concern our relations with other people and the state of our beliefs about ourselves and the world we live in. Certain dreams come directly from the High Self, though still interpreted by the subconscious. These tell us about our spiritual progress and sometimes give us foreknowledge of things to come.

There are telepathic dreams that come from people we know in this dream dimension, and even from situations that involve people we don't know. Often these deal with tragedy or danger because high emotions produce the extra *mana* that can activate telepathic awareness, but this is not always the case. In addition, there are dreams which consist of receiving instructions or information from more advanced entities, and dreams in which we travel in our *aka* body to another place in this or other dimensions.

In Huna different words describe different kinds of dreams. *Hihi'o* refers to hypnagogic-type dreams, those you have when half awake or half asleep, when dozing lightly, or when in a light trance. The code meaning is "to capture truth or reality." It is identical to the state a psychic uses to tune in to people or events.

In the ordinary language *kaha'ula* is usually associated with erotic dreams, but in the code it means "sacred place" or "soaring spirit." The idea here is that sexual dreams have to do with self-integration, a concept understood by the kahunas but seldom by others.

*Moemoea* is what would nowadays be called a "programmed" dream, one purposely sought or stimulated to help bring about a cherished desire. In the code it means "to set a line or net" and "to go straight toward something."

Finally, there was the *ho'ike na ka po*, "revelations of the night," dreams which are messages or guidance from the High Self or *aumakua*.

During the day the conscious self is more or less in control, and this physical dimension is perceived through the sensory information passed on by our subconscious. When we go to sleep, our subconscious gradually ceases to present the data from this dimension and begins to present data from another dimension. This other dimension does not have the same properties as the one we are more familiar with consciously. Note that the conscious mind is totally dependent on the subconscious for the presentation of experiential data. In order for the subconscious to present the data, it must use its own language of universal symbols, as well as memories of known experience. It is usually only the *representation* of the dream experience that we receive and not the experience itself. That is why so many dreams seem illogical from our point of view. If we want

to know what the experience was really all about,
we have to learn how to interpret the language of the
subconscious.

### INTERPRETING DREAMS

In learning to interpret your dreams, don't rely on
books of dream interpretation which dogmatically assert
that such and such an image always means such and
such a thing. There are some images and themes which
seem to be common to most if not all people, regardless of culture, but for the most part your dreams are
unique to you. As an example, if you like cats then a cat in
your dream could be a positive symbol, but if you hate
cats it could be negative. Likewise, for most people
a bridge might be a symbol of passing from one stage of
life to another, but if you are a civil engineer it might only
have to do with your job. Dreams can be interpreted
correctly only in the context of your own life, and while
books or other people can be very helpful for awhile, the
best interpretations will eventually come from you.

Just like sacred writings, your dreams can have many
levels of meaning. First look at the dream literally. If
you are planning a trip and you dream about a trip,
the dream might be giving you some information about
the trip itself. On the other hand, whether you are
planning a trip or not, the dream might be telling you
about a journey in consciousness. This would be the
allegorical level of interpretation, and its truth does not
negate the truth of the literal level. Many dreams
are just allegory or metaphor. If you dream that your head
falls off, you might be receiving the message that you are
"losing your head" over something. When death appears
in a dream, it is very seldom to be taken literally. In
nearly all cases it represents the death of a situation, a
condition, or a way of thinking. More accurately, it
presents a suggestion to create a symbolic death in order
to avoid a real one. The dream may be saying in effect,
"Change your way of life or lose it."

For the large majority of cases, the characters in your dreams represent you, or facets of you, or qualities you admire in another person, or distasteful qualities in yourself that you project onto others. Therefore, right after checking for the literal meaning of your relation to the characters (who may be relatives, friends, famous people, or strangers), pretend they are just mirrors for parts of yourself, and see what other insights you can get.

Even though your dreams are unique to you, there are some themes and symbols which are so common that they can apply to most people, unless they have a peculiar relevance to a particular life situation. The idea of a bridge representing a transition state has already been mentioned. Other symbols in this category are the crossing of a river, traveling a road or a path, walking down a highway, taking a train or a plane. Houses, hotels, and apartments often represent the beliefs you have about yourself and life, with the various rooms representing different compartments of thinking. A car very often means the physical body, the vehicle for your spirit, but it can also represent your whole self as you move through the world. Earthquakes can mean a sudden change in life, either about to happen or suggested, but they can also represent your feelings that your present situation is shaky. Animals can be aspects of your animal nature and birds can be spiritual messengers or higher thoughts. Water can be the subconscious self or psychic qualities, or emotions. Climbing usually refers to spiritual growth. Clothing reflects attitudes and habits, and in a dream something wrong with the way you dress can mean there is something wrong in the way you present yourself to the world.

Many people have recurrent dreams, that is, dreams that appear over and over again, either throughout life or merely during the course of a few weeks or days. These are exceptionally important because they denote the fact that your subconscious or superconscious is trying very hard to get a message across to you. When the message is understood and acted upon, at any level of awareness, such dreams disappear. Next in importance to recurrent dreams are recurrent themes. Once you get used to remembering your dreams you will frequently recall several dreams occurring during the course of a single night. If you record these dreams and compare the contents, you may find the same message repeated in different ways, as if to make sure you get it.

There are many techniques that can help you interpret your dreams. If you have achieved a good working relationship with your subconscious by using the pendulum, you can get meanings about your dreams through it. After all, it was your subconscious who related the dream. Sometimes you can wait until the next night and make a firm request before sleeping that a previous dream be made clear, or you can do the same thing during meditation. With practice, this will come in the form of another dream that is easier to interpret, or an inner voice that nicely explains what the dream is all about.

An in-depth method of dream interpretation using Gestalt techniques consists of acting out the role, mentally or physically, of each element in the dream to see what it reveals. In other words, you would take the part of each character in your dream and from that vantage point state how you feel and what your purpose is in being there, letting your imagination reel the information off the top of your head. After characters, you would continue to take the part of the other elements in the dream, for example the bridge, the water, the tree, an animal. You may at times be stunned by the insight this provides.

Another simpler method is to list the associations you make to particular elements of the dream. A white rose might remind you of purity, a lion of pride, or danger. When you complete the associations and apply them to your life, the interpretation may then immediately become clear to you.

These are general ideas, of course, and you may want to follow them up by referring to books that deal more fully with interpretation.

An unusual but quite effective method for understanding dreams is to use "programmed interpretation." To make this work well, you take a particular dream interpretation book or a symbolic system such as astrology, numerology, Tarot and firmly tell your subconscious to channel your dreams through those symbols. You have to become very familiar with the symbols and keep them for ready reference by your bedside, and you must keep repeating the suggestion often. Within a short time most, if not all, of your dreams will use the symbolism of your choice. Then interpretation becomes mainly a matter of conscious reference to the symbols.

This section on interpretation would not be complete without a word on nightmares. Actually, nightmares are nothing more than symbolic representations of intense inner conflict. Sometimes the conflict is between your body and the substances you put in it, but more often it is a conflict of emotions and ideas. Nightmares usually come only after a prolonged period of conscious repression of the issue. They are a way for your subconscious or High Self to say "HEY!!" They get your attention. If the nightmares are recurrent, give yourself permission or get some help to deal with the issues involved, and the nightmares will cease. Drugs to suppress dreaming are *not* the answer.

### REMEMBERING DREAMS

A fair number of people have trouble remembering their dreams, because of simple lack of attention, conditioning that says dreams are unimportant or dangerous to fool with, or because of bad experiences with nightmares as a child. Dreams are a tool, however, and to use them you have to remember them. Here are a few ways that can help with this, no matter what your experience has been.

As you go to sleep, tell yourself that you want to remember your dreams. Be firm, and reinforce the point by keeping paper and pen close by your bed so that you can record dreams as they become available. Depending on the time available, you can write them out in detail or just make a few brief notes. The writing and the intention will improve your dream memory.

If you wake up in the morning without recalling that you have dreamed, gently change position in the bed without getting up. Try several positions, and just lie quietly in each for a few moments with your awareness open. Often a forgotten dream will spring to mind when your body assumes the sleeping position you had while dreaming it.

Read about dreams and think about them a lot. This conscious attention will in itself direct your subconscious to bring more of them to your awareness. Along similar lines, try your mind at waking dreams. Sit or lie down and close your eyes, letting yourself drift into a state of relaxed and passive attention, and just observe the contents of your mind. You may experience some images having to do with affairs of the day, or you may even have no images at all for awhile. Sooner or later, however, you will experience a true dream while wide awake. It will "feel" different from your normal thinking, and it will seem to be spontaneous, unexpected, and probably irrelevant. You can interpret waking dreams in the same way as a sleeping dream, and they will help you become more aware of those dreams, too.

### CONCLUSION

I make no pretension at having exhausted the subject of dreams in this short chapter. We have not even touched on programmed dreams, healing dreams, teaching dreams, group dreaming, lucid dreams, shamanistic dreams, and many other forms. The purpose here is to get you started on an adventure into inner space. By paying attention to your dreams, you will gain valuable knowledge about yourself, where you are going, the faults you have to correct, and you may receive excellent advice on all kinds of matters. You will also be improving your psychic abilities.

The language of dreams is akin to the language of telepathy and clairvoyance. It is your subconscious that is speaking in all cases. Over a period of time you will learn the language and be able to interpret messages received from many psychic sources. By following the advice of dreams for self-growth, we open ourselves up to the acquisition of further psychic abilities and spiritual knowledge.

A great many of mankind's most valuable artistic and scientific achievements have become manifest because people paid attention to their dreams. There is no need to spend a third of your life unconscious. Live that third. You dream for a purpose. Find out what it is.

# 12

## Practical Techniques

Meditation is one of the oldest known ways for human
beings to alter conditions of mind, body, and cir-
cumstance and to explore realms of experience beyond
the self. It is used in all religions and esoteric organiza-
tions the world over. The word basically means "to think
about," but in practice it is a little more complicated
than that. In Yoga the process is broken down into three
stages. First there is concentration, or the directing of the
attention to the object. Then there is meditation
proper, the continuous application of the attention to
the object. Most people who engage in meditation stop
here. The next, more advanced stage called contemplation, is identification with the object.

A good deal of confusion exists today about meditation because there are two widely varying schools of
thought on the subject, as well as variations in the
definition of terms. Disciplines such as Zen and Yoga
put the emphasis on what might be called "passive"
meditation. In this the mind is swept clean of all thoughts

in order to clear the way for attunement with the Cosmic Mind. This leads to samadhi or satori, a blissful, enlightening union with the Infinite, and all good things like love, happiness, prosperity, health, and psychic powers happen automatically along the way.

The exponents of "active" meditation include the Judeao-Christian religions, "positive thinking" practitioners, hypnotists, occultists, and the many teachers of mind control techniques. In this type of meditation, the mind is actively filled with the specific qualities or events that one wants to make manifest.

### THE HUNA PRACTICE

The kahunas used both methods. Their word for passive meditation was *nalu* and for active meditation it was *no'ono'o*. For both types they used a four-step process:

> Awareness, *ike*, the directing of attention to the object of meditation.
>
> Release or elimination, *kala*, of anything that distracts from the object of meditation, like doubts or tension.
>
> Highly focused attention, or concentration, *makia*.
>
> Continued focus combined with feeling, *manawa*, until the purpose of the meditation is achieved. It includes the sending and/or receiving of energy.

The use of active or passive meditation depends on the purpose of the meditation and the personality of the meditator. The kahunas are always more concerned with effects than technique. The best technique is the one that works for you.

### POSTURE

To many persons the word meditation conjures up an image of bare feet, long hair, a robe, and the "lotus" position popularized by Indian yogis. It may be more comfortable to meditate with your shoes off if they are tight, but otherwise it doesn't matter. Most Buddhist meditators are shaved bald, so hair length makes no difference either. A loose-fitting robe is quite comfortable, but as long as your clothes aren't cutting off circulation, you don't have to change them. As for what position to move your limbs into, one of the earliest and greatest yogis, Patanjali, said to choose a position that is comfortable, but not so comfortable that you fall asleep easily. It is possible to meditate while lying down, sitting, standing on your feet or head, walking, or even while working at a monotonous job. The most important point is be comfortable enough so that your body sensations don't distract you from your meditation. Then come considerations of convenience, your own state of advancement, and the purpose of the meditation. If you are new to meditation, I would suggest a comfortable chair with a fairly straight back or sitting on a pillow on the floor with your back against a wall.

### VISUALIZATION

Visualization is an ability that is greatly misunderstood. Many people who are actually good visualizers think they aren't because they expect it to be something quite different from what they are doing. So when meditation instructions call for visualization, these people just give up.

Everyone can visualize, even people born blind. If you have ever recalled a memory image, however fleeting, or if you have ever had a visual dream, then you can visualize. Now, some people use it more than others and can describe it better, but that just makes them more skilled because of practice. Visualization, while a great asset to meditation, is only one of a number of abilities that are used, and not an essential one at that. So if you already visualize well, that's fine; if you think you don't, you don't have to worry about it. Just do the best you can and put more emphasis on your other abilities, like auditory and kinesthetic (feeling) imagination, and you may find you are better at those than the visualizers.

## Relaxation

Much of what passes for meditation is nothing more than good old relaxation. This is true of any so-called meditation system that teaches you no more than the fixation of attention on an image, a sound, a feeling, or an object, without eventually taking you beyond that simple fixation of attention. True meditation involves an increase in awareness, skill, knowledge, or experience. Relaxation is healthy; it is calming. It is an excellent *prelude* to meditation, but it is not meditation itself.

When convenient, it is a good idea to do a relaxation exercise before meditation because it helps to eliminate distracting tension, calms your emotions, and clears your mind. Fixing your attention on anything will tend to produce a relaxing effect, but here I will recommend a breathing technique. Just take four slow, deep breaths to oxygenate your blood and increase your alertness, and then keep your attention on the natural flow of your breathing until you feel comfortably relaxed. If you have another method you like better, use it.

## Centered Awareness

This is a basic development exercise which provides a foundation for many other techniques and which itself helps to increase your sense of confidence and balance.

> 1. Imagine there is a point of light within yourself, at your navel, your contact with a Source of unlimited energy, power and love.
>
> 2. Imagine this light vibrating at a very high frequency and slowly radiating outward in all directions through your body, until you are surrounded on all sides by a field of vibrating light.
>
> 3. Imagine that each time you inhale, even more light is radiated and each time you exhale the light around you gets more intense and vibrates more strongly.

4. Maintain your awareness of this surrounding light for as long as possible or practicable.

This technique may be practiced at any time, anywhere, with your eyes open or closed.

## MINDSHIELD

Many psychoreligious systems around the world have the concept of a "white light of protection." The kahunas call it *la'a kea*, the sacred white light. It is good to build up the habit of surrounding yourself with the white light before going into meditation. Some systems recommend it because otherwise you might be susceptible to "negative entities" just waiting to jump into an unwary meditator. The Huna reason is much more pragmatic and reasonable. The purpose is to shut out or neutralize unconscious negative thoughts and emotions from other people, until you are so strong in your own thoughts that you can't be affected by others.

1. Surround yourself with light.

2. Imagine that this surrounding field of light has the power to dissolve and neutralize any negativity before it even reaches you.

3. Mentally say the word *Shield!* several times, and tell yourself that this keyword will automatically start the protection process in the future any time you need it.

4. Use your breathing (as described in the first technique) to strengthen the shield effect as you feel it is necessary.

It is a fact that the negative emotional states and thoughts of others—friends or strangers—may upset us at times. Our mood changes and sudden pains do not always originate within ourselves, though we only react to that which we are potentially sensitive to in our own thinking. Here is a way to block out such negative input and remain true to the way you want to be.

You might try imagining a beam of sunlight shining down on you from directly overhead, something like the beam you see breaking through the clouds on occasion. You are in the center of this beam and it surrounds you on all sides. You feel its warmth penetrating right through your body, energizing every cell, and you know you are completely safe and secure within that light. While it protects you, it is cleansing you of all negative thoughts and feelings and chasing away any undesirable thoughts that may be directed toward you. Nothing that is not good can penetrate the light.

This simple protective technique will serve for the vast majority of people, but there are many possible variations. You can imagine your body or aura being filled with light through a cord that connects you to your High Self. Instead of using light, you can mentally flip a switch that charges you with protective energy. Some people see themselves inside a transparent, unbreakable glass egg. And there are those who only need to sense their High Self hovering over them like a guardian angel. It doesn't matter so much how you establish a protection so long as you do it.

Often you will find that pains like headaches will disappear or lessen immediately and moods will lighten when you use this technique. It is very good for use in rooms, buildings, or other areas where you feel uncomfortable without knowing why, or around people who have the knack of upsetting you unreasonably.

If you find that this technique makes no difference in how you feel, then you can be certain that your upset is caused by your own thinking, and you can work on resolving that in other ways.

#### How to Influence Others in a Positive Way

It is one thing to protect yourself from the negative influence of others, and quite another to exert a positive influence yourself. Each has its purpose and place. Here is a technique to try when you are ready to be more assertive.

1. Surround yourself with a field of light.

2. Choose a color appropriate to your purpose. For example, pink for friendliness, green for cooperation, blue for calming, etc. There are no right or wrong colors. What matters most is what feels best to you.

3. Imagine this color flowing out from you to penetrate and surround other people, objects that you or they use, and/or environments in which you or they live, work, or play. You may have the color take the form of pure light, a fog, or even spray paint, if that helps you get the mental picture.

4. At the same time, mentally affirm with strong desire that the color is having the effect you want.

You can use this to improve conditions at home or at work, for repairing relationships, for protecting people, places, or things that you are concerned about, or influencing people in beneficial ways. *Note this well:* You cannot control others by doing this; you can only influence them to the degree that they subconsciously accept your projection. They still have free will, but the more positive and beneficial your influence, the more likely they are to respond.

### How to Neutralize Unwanted Suggestions

Unwanted, negative suggestions or statements that tend to increase your own fears, anxieties, and self-doubts can come from other people, advertisements, or even your own mind and mouth, and they can adversely affect your health, emotions, and sense of self-confidence if you accept them without question. Usually they are stated as facts, when actually they are only opinions. You do not have to accept such suggestions. Here is a way to counteract them.

1. Become aware that a statement just made may act as a negative suggestion (this will take some practice in actually paying attention to what is being said or read).

2. Immediately, aloud or silently, say to yourself, "That's not true, I don't accept it, cancel that!"

3. Aloud or silently, replace it with a positive opposite

statement of your own, a statement that you *want* to believe is true even if you don't completely believe it as yet.

4. Use the mindshield technique if the negative suggestion is accompanied by a negative emotion.

Once you begin this, you may find yourself using it quite frequently for awhile, which will show you how much negative thinking there is in the world. Be sure to pay attention to your own speech and thoughts, because negative suggestions given to yourself by yourself are even more distructive than those given by others. This technique may also be used to neutralize negative criticism.

### How to Deal with Emotional Upsets

One of the great secrets of the body is that it is physiologically impossible to feel strong negative emotions when your muscles are completely relaxed. The next time you are emotionally upset or even overly excited, you can try the following technique.

1. Surround yourself with light.

2. Lightly press the fingertip pads of both hands together without your palms touching.

3. As you breathe in, imagine that light from your center is flowing to the areas of your body that feel most tense. This may take some practice. You may find it easier at first if you try at the end of your inhalation rather than during it.

4. As you exhale, imagine that all the emotional energy is being released into your surrounding field of light, there to be dissolved and neutralized, leaving your muscles limp and relaxed.

One to five minutes of the above exercise should be sufficient for you to relax enough so that you can face your situation with a much calmer attitude. The same technique can be used for general relaxation at any time. Slow, deep breathing helps the process.

*Practical Techniques*

## How to Apply First Aid Healing Energy

All of us have the ability to generate healing energy with our hands and use it for ourselves and others. To become a well-trained healer takes considerable study and practice, but you can produce beneficial results right now with what you have. This technique is best for minor aches and pains like headaches, cuts and bruises, sore muscles, stomach aches, and the like. It will result in lessening or disappearance of the pain and a speedier healing.

> 1. Surround yourself with light. As you breathe in, imagine more light from your center pouring into your hands. As you breathe out, imagine this light pouring out of your palms and/or fingers.
>
> 2. Rub your palms briskly to further stimulate the flow of energy. You may even be able to feel the output if you hold your hands facing each other.
>
> 3. Hold your hands over the affected area, either touching it or a couple inches above it. Imagine and desire the energy to penetrate the area and neutralize the pain. Imagining the energy as a color is very helpful. Repeat steps 1 and 2 to keep the energy flowing.
>
> 4. When you have finished—when the pain is gone or diminished—you may rinse your hands, shake your fingers, or touch the floor to discharge any negative energy you may have picked up.

Remember that this is first aid. Do whatever else is necessary to treat the problem.

## Conscious Observer

There are innumerable ways to meditate, and just as many reasons for doing it. Here is a type of passive meditation simple and basic enough for beginners, and yet profound enough for advanced masters. Its purpose is to develop inner awareness and allow you to explore the content and structure of your mind. After practicing some of the exercises already given, you will see how this differs from active meditation.

> 1. In a comfortable position, surround yourself with light, take a deep breath, and close your eyes.

> 2. Now focus your attention on your natural breathing pattern for awhile until your emotions are calm and your body is relaxed. Then direct your focus inward, keeping your attention on the thoughts, sounds, images and feelings that appear in your mind. Observe how they change and shift, appear and disappear.

> 3. Maintain your role as a conscious observer. Put aside any judgments, criticisms, or expectations. Whatever does happen is supposed to happen. You may experience memories, visions, voices, sensations, something else, or nothing at all. Observe, remember as much as you can, avoid interpretations, and stay as consciously aware as you can at all times.

> 4. When you are finished, just take a deep breath and open your eyes.

If you fall asleep, that's all right, but aim toward maintaining awareness. It is helpful to write down your experiences, but this is not necessary. Take as long as you like, and modify the process as you desire. For instance, you could ask a question before you start and relate your experience to that, or you could request contact with your High Self or God Within and do the same. There is no right or wrong way to do this meditation.

# 13

## Creative Meditation

Among all the methods used by the kahunas, none
are so potent in my opinion as a class known as *tikis*. A
*tiki* (*ki'i* in Hawaiian) is familiar to many Westerners as a
carved figure, usually of wood. In kahuna usage it
refers to a mental power image of which the physical
figure is only a representation. There are many *tikis* for
many purposes, and they range from the very simple
to the extremely complex. In this chapter I am going to
present simple *tikis* for everyday use and one that is
somewhat more complicated for those who wish to explore this concept a little further.

### Building Thought Forms

The first type of active creative meditation we will
consider is the actual building of thought forms. This has
been called everything from prayer to magic, but it
really is no more than imagining what you want and be-
lieving that it will happen, either through your own
efforts or with the help of something greater than

yourself. However, another important ingredient
that many systems neglect is energy, *mana*, the life force
that actually makes the thought form a reality. Following is one Huna method for practising this kind of
meditation.

Prepare yourself for meditation as before, only this
time take about ten deep breaths and turn the white light
into a highly charged energy field filling you as well
as surrounding you. If you can develop a sensation of
tingling when you do this, that's good, but in the beginning all you need is the intent. At the same time, ask
for contact with your High Self, God Within, the spirit of
Christ, or whatever greater being you acknowledge.

Next bring your cupped hands in front of you about
waist high and a foot or so apart. Imagine that the light/
energy that fills you is pouring out of your palms and
forming an energy ball that you are holding in your hands.
Rubbing your hands together first will stimulate the
flow of energy and help you get the feeling of it. Now the
ball is ready to be "programmed."

As a first exercise, think of someone you know who
needs help. Imagine the person's form in the energy ball
between your hands, and imagine him receiving the
energy and being healed and happy. Keep this up till you
get a clear sense of something happening, even if
you're not sure what. Then release the thought form to
do its work. There are a number of ways to do this,
such as tossing the ball upward or pressing it into your
body and telling your inner or higher self to take it and do
what is necessary. The ancient kahunas would raise
their hands and blow the ball upward, ending the meditation session with a prayer like *Amama, ua noa, lele
wale akua la!* ("It is ended, the *mana* is released, let it
manifest.") The most important thing at this point is to
maintain a feeling of confidence that your higher self will
carry out your request.

The same basic technique is used if you have a
personal problem that you want resolved. This time,

when you have built your ball of energy, picture yourself in it, happy and healthy, with the problem resolved. Use your imagination to make it as real as possible. Feel the satisfaction and happiness that will come from having the condition fulfilled. The more reality you can put into it, the stronger your thought form will be. When you have made it as strong as you can, release it and bring the session to a definite end.

The more a desired condition differs from your present one, and the more doubts or fears you have concerning it, the more often and intensely you will have to do the meditation. Once a day is a bare minimum; the more often the better. Keep it up until the condition is fulfilled. If you change your mind, be sure to do a special meditation to cancel what you were programming, or the energy you put into it will continue to bring related effects into your life.

## Passive Creative Meditation

In the active type of meditation, you actively create in imagination the kind of conditions you want. In this passive kind of meditation, you seek to enter a state of consciousness in which the right things happen automatically, without your having to imagine specifically the results you want.

Passive creative meditation takes a considerable amount of trust, which is why it is followed by a relatively small number of people. In *no'ono'o* you must trust that the results will come about as you have imagined them, but in *nalu* you must trust that the results will come about even if you don't imagine them.

As with active creative meditation, the use of the white light and relaxation exercises are strongly recommended as a prelude. After that the first step is to pick an object of meditation. This is usually a concept rather than a thing or a condition. For instance, where a *no'ono'o* meditator might direct his attention to a particular type of job, a certain amount of money, the healing of a specific condition, or having a good relationship, the *nalu* meditator would pick the concepts of employment, wealth, health, or love.

The second step is to concentrate on the concept, to keep your mind on it during the whole period of meditation (which could be a few minutes or all day long). This includes letting yourself think about what the concept really is, what it means, how it appears in the world, how it could be better, what it feels like, and so on.

The third step is to be aware of your doubts and fears concerning the concept as they come up. You seek the roots of them if you can. Then you eliminate them by turning your attention away from them once they've made their appearance. Turn your full attention back to the positive aspects of the concept you are meditating on. Sometimes you can argue the doubts and fears out of existence, and sometimes you simply have to crush them and refuse to entertain them. Then you trust that your continued focus on the concept you've chosen will itself get rid of those fears and doubts. If physical tension occurs during the focus, then you ease it in whatever way is appropriate and immediately go back to your focus.

The final phase occurs when the positive aspects of the concept fill your mind so completely that your thoughts, feelings, and behavior are all aligned with it, and you have made an identification with it. When that begins to happen, you will find your life changing accordingly. If love was your object of focus, you will not only find yourself becoming more loving, but you will find yourself attracting friends and deeper relationships of just the right kind, in what seems to be an effortless way. If your focus has been wealth, you will get many opportunities to earn or receive money that will come "out of the blue." At this stage you are radiating an attractive energy that draws to you the best available equivalent that the universe has to offer.

By using this kind of meditation, you are putting complete faith in your High Self. You are affirming that "I have my perfect job (income, relationship, lifestyle, etc.)" while leaving it up to your higher self as to exactly what that will be. It usually turns out far better than you would ever have imagined by yourself. However, you may have to go through some dark periods as your doubts and fears make their way out of your system, and this is where the need for trust is so vital.

Some people consider that the highest form of this kind of meditation is to focus on God, or God's love, God's abundance, God's power, and so on. The only way you will find out is to try it yourself.

## MEADOW, FOREST, MOUNTAIN

Now we will deal with a type of creative meditation designed to develop powers of concentration and teach many valuable things about oneself. It uses what we call *tikis*, created images of sight, sound, and feeling. Out of many possibilities, we will use a meadow, a forest, and a mountain.

After taking up your meditation position and doing your relaxation exercise, proceed with the following:

1. Imagine yourself in a meadow in springtime. A stream cuts across the meadow and you are seated beside it. Build this image in as detailed a way as possible, using every one of your senses. Feel the grass with your fingers. Dip a hand into the stream. Is there a breeze? Is it cool or warm? Do you hear birds or insects? Are there flowers? Can you smell them? Are you alone in the meadow? Is this a place you have been to before or seen in a picture, or is it brand new? Explore this meadow carefully with all your senses. This is going to be your place for re-attuning yourself to your own nature.

When you are ready, take a deep breath and bring yourself out of meditation to consider the experience. Was it pleasant, or did you experience things you didn't like? The meadow represents one part of your mind. Your conscious mind creates the overall meadow pattern by design or intent, but your subconscious fills in most of the details. Anything that was imperfect in the meadow is a reflection of imperfections in your thinking.

If you can correct the imperfections in the meadow by using your creative imagination during meditation (e.g., cutting the grass if it is too high to permit you to see anything), you will be taking a giant step toward correcting the problems they represent in your daily life. A careful analysis of everything in the meadow as if the whole thing were a reflection of yourself will increase your self-knowledge greatly. Unless your thinking is too rigid, you will probably notice changes in the meadow every time you meditate on it. This, of course, reflects the changes in you.

2. During another session, imagine that you are walking through a forest. Again, build up the detail and see, feel, hear everything you can. If you find berries, taste them. Note whether you are on a path. Is the forest peaceful or foreboding? Do the trees seem friendly or threatening? Are there animals? How do you react to them? Analyze this experience as you did the one above. If you are beset by hidden fears, they will show up in this scene. Be sure you realize this is *your* creation. Regardless of what happens, it is only a mental experience. If something starts to chase you, stop and chase it back. By overcoming any dangers here, you will learn to overcome them in the physical world.

3. In a third session, imagine that you are climbing a mountain, at the top of which is a building. Give yourself a specific time period for this, like two or five minutes, and experience it in great detail as you did the others. In particular you want to note whether the climb was difficult or easy and, if there were obstacles, what they were like and what you did about them. You will also want to note what kind of building you found at

the top and all the details concerning it. Of course, if you never made it to the top or inside the building in the time allowed, that is important, too. Your subconscious knows how much time is available for the experience. This meditation represents goals and objectives and how you stand in relation to them.

Aside from gaining self-knowledge, one of the main purposes in practising these meditations is to make each of the scenes so beautiful that you will enjoy going back again and again. This by itself will refresh and eneregize your whole being. Do not be surprised if the experience turns into a dreamlike sequence in which events occur that you did not consciously anticipate. Follow them through and remember that; while you may not control the events, you can always control your reaction to them. You will learn many things in this way.

## The Garden Meditation

*Introduction to the Garden.* Huna teaches that every aspect of our outer experience has its counterpart in thought, and that each of these can influence the other. In other words, your thoughts reflect your experience and your experience reflects your thoughts. Since by changing your experience you can change your thoughts, so by changing your thoughts you can change your experience. The garden *tiki* (*waena*) is a way of organizing your thoughts into a specific pattern that gives you new insights about your present experience and serves as a tool for change and growth. The very name of this *tiki* is a full description of what it can do: *waena* means garden or center, a place of growth and a way of centering.

The image, as you have probably guessed, is that of a garden, your own private, secluded place that is as unique as your own identity. To form it, you may draw upon the memory of a place you have visited physically, the memory of pictures or descriptions of a garden that

147

you like or you can invent your own completely. In practice, most people use a combination of these and usually start by allowing the subconscious to come up with a garden image full blown, as it were.

*Establishing the Garden.* Establishing a garden *tiki* is as easy as day-dreaming. All you really have to do is think of a garden, let one appear in your imagination, modify it consciously if you want to, and make the experience as real as you can. It is no more difficult than that. Relaxation is helpful, but even if you don't feel very relaxed to begin with, the process of getting imaginatively involved in the garden will relax you in itself.

Formal hypnosis or formal meditation are not necessary at all, but they can be useful in helping you relax and focus your attention. Having someone guide you through the process may also be helpful, but this is not necessary, either. It is the *doing* that is important, not how you do it. Use whatever works.

If you feel you are not very visual, practice with the garden will help to develop this ability. However, the ability to visualize mentally is not a critical factor. It doesn't matter if your first attempts to "see" the garden produce only fuzzy or vague outlines, or even no visual aspect at all. Complete imagination includes imaginary sound, touch, smell, taste, and emotional feeling. If your imagination is not yet well developed visually, it certainly will be in other ways.

In the beginning it is a good idea to do this exercise alone while sitting or lying down in a quiet place where you will be undisturbed (unless someone is helping you through the process). After some practice you will find yourself able to do it virtually any time in any place. It doesn't matter if your eyes are open or closed—some people find it easier one way, some the other—but I would suggest developing the skill to do it both ways.

For those who would like a standard technique for establishing and reproducing the garden, the following has been used successfully by many.

1. Take a deep breath, close your eyes, and relax. Think of a garden, let an image or idea of it form in your mind, even if it isn't clear yet. If you wish, imagine yourself traveling to the garden in some way.

2. Focus your attention to see three things in the garden as clearly as you can (such as a flower, a fountain, and a tree); hear three things (such as a bird, flowing water, and the rustle of leaves); and touch three things (such as the ground beneath your feet, a petal, and a handful of soil). You may also add taste and smell if you like.

3. Now explore your garden. Find out what kinds of plants are growing there; check their condition and that of the soil; examine the water supply; note how the garden is organized; be aware of anything else of interest. At this time you can use the garden in any way you know how. You may find it useful to establish a reference point of some kind—a fountain, a particular plant, or a statue—to use as an inner landmark so you can return quickly to the garden at any time.

4. When you have finished with the garden for this time, generate a strong, positive emotion, bless your garden, come back to your physical body awareness, take a deep breath, and open your eyes.

*Using the Garden.* Here are some practical ways to use the garden *tiki*:

*Relaxation.* Whenever you feel uptight or tense, take some time out and go to your garden for a sort of "mini-vacation." Give yourself some space in your garden to do whatever you like to relax (I enjoy just lying in a hammock). Be there with all your senses. In a few moments or minutes your physical body will reflect the relaxation of your *tiki* body.

*Interpretation.* At one level the garden represents your present state of mind, so everything in it can be interpreted like symbols in a dream. The symbols will be your own, though, and rigid interpretations from a book or someone else's philosophy will be very limiting. Nevertheless, dream books can give you ideas for interpretation, and these general guidelines might be helpful: a lack of water (in a plant or soil) may mean that you are withholding or suppressing your emotions; buds on flowers that won't open may mean a fear of growth or of growing up; fences or walls may mean inner blocks of doubt or fear; weeds may indicate negative thoughts. Translate the condition of your garden in a literal way and apply that to your outer life. Any interpretation is only as valid as you feel it to be. Trust your own feelings before those of someone else. The value of interpreting is that you can discover areas in your outer life where making changes could be beneficial.

*Maintenance.* Your garden grows and changes as you do. If you are in a happy state when you "go to your garden," the garden will reflect that. If you are in a confused, unhappy, or fearful state, it will reflect that, too. However, if you change or improve the condition of your garden image, that will affect your state of mind, body, and emotions. One good practice is to go to your garden regularly, say for a few minutes in the morning and again just before bedtime, and check it out. See what condition everything is in, and if you find something that needs improvement (such as weeding, dry soil, wilted plants), then fix it by whatever means come to mind. In your garden you can have anything available that you want for taking care of it. For this exercise you need not know the significance of the condition that needs improvement. All you have to do is work in the garden, and your subconscious or body-mind will take care of the rest.

*Helpers.* It can be very useful, as well as more fun, to have helpers in your garden. These can be considered as laborers or expert gardeners and will work completely under your direction (since they are aspects of your own mind). Because of beliefs, fears and doubts, it is sometimes difficult to make changes in your garden, even though it is a process of the imagination. Creating helpers adds to your psychic energy and makes the change process easier. The helpers can take things out of your garden, add to it, or reorganize what is there already. While you can use humans as helpers, many people find it more enjoyable to have menehunes, elves, dwarves, devas, or the like. Just want the helpers to be there when you need them, and they will appear.

*Resolution.* Everything in your life is reflected in your garden. If you have a problem of some kind in your outer life—physical, mental, social, vocational, spiritual, or whatever—go to your garden and ask to see this problem as it is represented there. In a moment or so you will get a spontaneous image which is that problem as it appears in your garden. Sometimes the symbolism will be very clear, and at other times it will be obscure. However, this is another case where you need not interpret. All you have to do is correct the situation at hand in your garden. As simple as this sounds, it is far-reaching and powerful in its effects. A few examples of how it has been used will make it clearer:

> A man suffering from anxiety attacks went to his garden and asked where the fear was. He saw a huge, thick bramble bush with giant thorns. He tried to chop it down, but it was too tough, so he gathered a large team of helpers and together they tore it down, took out the roots, pulverized the plant for compost, replowed the ground, and planted courage, confidence, and strength. The attacks stopped.

> A woman with a toothache that didn't respond well to medication went to her garden, asked to see the problem, and found a telephone pole with a live wire down and sparking on the ground near the edge of her garden. She called in an expert repairman who fixed the line. Shortly afterwards, the pain in her tooth was gone without any more medication. (Note: This took care of the pain, but not the physical condition of the tooth).

> A woman concerned about a relationship asked to see this in her garden and found a fruit tree. As nothing

appeared to be wrong with the tree, she asked it what it needed. The tree replied that it needed love, patience, and understanding, so she sprinkled these around the base of the tree like fertilizer. Her relationship improved.

*Response.* The last example above shows how a woman used the response technique in her garden. Your garden is a magical place that does not need to follow the rules of physical reality. Changes there can occur instantly, and everything can talk. If you are seeking information about your life or about what you are experiencing in your garden, you can simply ask, and you will get a response. You can talk to flowers, trees, birds, helpers. These conversations can be used for interpretation, insight, and guidance.

*Guides.* Another kind of guidance comes in the form of personal guides, if you want them. To invite a guide, stand in your garden and call out for one to appear, and in a moment or so he or she will be there. You can allow your inner self to send the best type of guide for your current need, or you can specify the type of guide you wish (such as a health guide, a prosperity guide, a wise old man. When the guide appears, give a greeting and take a moment to see him clearly, hear him make some movement or sound, and touch his hand or clothing. Then have a conversation. *Do not let the guide give you orders or tell you what you should do.* A proper guide only gives advice and leaves the final decision up to you. If you seem to receive orders or "shoulds" from a guide, you are distorting the response with your conscious mind, so don't blame the guide. You are not meant to be a puppet. The guides are there to serve you, not to command you.

They usually take a human form, but some people will come up with animal or alien guides, or mythological characters. Do not get caught up in trying to figure out who or what the guides really are. As long as the advice is good, the origin doesn't really matter. Also, don't expect the guides to be infallible about predicting events. All of this is taking place in your mind and the guides know as much about the future as you do, thought they may be able to express what they know more clearly.

*The Gardens of Others.* Your thoughts and emotions are being broadcast outward at this very moment, whether you will it or not, to every human being on earth. Most will have no discernible response to that broadcast, some will respond by taking part in your life in some fashion or another, and very, very few will be aware, if they choose, of the source of that broadcast. These might choose to make a conscious response that will influence you in turn.

We are all living in a telepathic sea of thought and emotional energy, but we have various kinds of automatic filters that screen out thoughts and feelings that are not compatible with our beliefs. Therefore, no one can "program" our minds against our will, although it is possible to sway our thinking in the way that a salesman might. What I am about to share is not a telepathic invasion of another person's mind—that is quite impossible—but it is a conscious response to what another may be broadcasting, and it is an attempt to influence the broadcaster in a positive way.

The approach is simply this: in order to exert a helpful influence on someone else, go to that person's garden as it appears in your mind. Once there, use any of the techniques given to effect a beneficial change. Now, in doing this you are actually working with your personal interpretation of the other's telepathic broadcasting. Everything that happens in the garden takes place in your mind and nowhere else. However, it is also broadcast out from you to the other person concerned, and he then has the opportunity to respond to it, or not at a subconscious level. The more obviously beneficial the change, the more likely the person is to respond, but there are no guarantees. This is a way of offering help, not forcing it.

Garden healing of others has the great advantage of allowing you to bypass their conscious doubts and of being able to work at a distance. Although you are not going into another person's mind and you are not trying to do anything against his will, it is still more ethical and courteous first to inform the other or, ask permission whenever possible. In the case of young children and pets (or anyone for that matter), you can always "go to their garden" and ask something you find in that garden whether it is all right for you to make any changes there.

Assuming that there is such a thing as group consciousness, it may be possible to tune into the garden of a particular group and work on that. This is speculative, but worth investigating. It may be that the best approach is one group working on the garden of another group. Possible groups to work on could be cities, states, and countries. Unless there are criteria by which to judge results, however, all such work has to remain speculative.

By beneficially changing another's garden as it appears in your mind, you are working on a symbolic and nonjudgmental level which allows the other to respond in the most natural and unbiased way. At the same time you will be altering your view of the other.

*Teaching the Garden Tiki.* For those who wish to teach others the garden *tiki* for self-development or therapy, here are a few guidelines:

1. In using suggestion to help others to establish a garden, avoid being too specific about what they are going to experience. The less structure from you the better, although you may have to coax them into experiencing plants, soil, and water. The more you allow them freedom in developing their garden, the more accurately it will reflect their life and state of mind.

2. Prepare to be very flexible. In all likelihood you will get many surprises as people describe their gardens and what happens in them. Often it may not be what *you*

think a garden should be like or what should happen
in it. Remember that this is the magical world of the mind
of others. If you are helping them to deal with the
images they conjure up, act like a guide. That is, give
ideas and advice only, but let them make the decisions
as to what to do. Sometimes they might not at the
moment want to deal with what they find. Respect that.

3. No matter how little a person experiences, be encouraging. There is no right or wrong way to do this, no
right or wrong experience. Be patient, use more relaxation if need be, and be willing to spend more time in
developing the visual, auditory, and kinesthetic
channels.

4. If people begin to get negative feedback in the
form of demons, witches, monsters, etc. in the garden,
then either have them take a deep breath and open their
eyes, or have them deal with the negatives in some
appropriate, successful way. What you do will depend on
how much fear is present. In any case, help them
realize that these are nothing more than mental images,
projections of their own fears and doubts, which are subject to change and mastery. The monsters can be
destroyed, made into friends, or transformed, according
to what their creator (not you) believes will be most
effective.

5. Even without a hypnotic or meditative induction,
some people will tend to trance out just after they get into
the garden. In other words, they will seem to fall
asleep, go into an amnesiac state, or start wandering into
other images. It is your job to keep them in the garden
until they accomplish something. If you can't do that,
don't use this *tiki*.

Many "mindworkers" have invented structured
imagery or *tikis* for various purposes. There is nothing
sacred about them, whether they are religious in nature
or not, just as none of the kahuna *tikis* are considered
sacred and not to be changed. They are only tools.
Feel free, then, to make up your own or modify any you

find to suit your own purposes. The only thing that is sacred and cannot be changed is the infinity within you.

### FOCUSING

There is no one right kind of meditation. Passive meditation is not "better" than active, nor vice versa. Creative meditation is not better than pure awareness meditation, nor the other way around. No technique or system is intrinsically better than another. Different ones serve different purposes. Some techniques may be more effective for some people at certain times and places, but no technique is best for everyone all the time.

In this chapter we have given only a few techniques in the creative mode. There are probably hundreds more. Experiment with these and give yourself the freedom to experiment with others. However, be cautioned that the effectiveness of every single meditation technique depends on one thing—the degree of concentration you apply to its purpose. What counts is not the number of times you meditate, not when you do it, not how well you follow the form, not how "hard" you concentrate. It is degree of concentration, which means length of focus free of doubts. If you meditate on what you want every morning for twenty minutes and spend sixteen hours doubting that you can get it, your results will be disappointing.

Also if you focus on getting a good job for five minutes every night and don't give it another practical thought during the day, your chances are pretty slim. Be open to creative ideas and impulses that may come to you at any time, whether in your own mind, through the words or actions of others, or by your being drawn to certain places. The Source of creativity can work miracles, but miracles usually happen in practical ways.

# 14

## Spiritual Integration

In Huna terms spiritual integration and action are the conscious joining of the three selves—the conscious, subconscious, and superconscious—and the carrying out of one's highest purpose in life.When the three selves are joined in an earthly existence, the result is called *Kanaloa*, the companion of God. In ancient Hawaiian legend, the god Kanaloa and the great god Kane were drinking buddies, and they used to go from island to island creating springs of fresh water (a symbol of life and wealth). By tradition Kanaloa was a god of the sea (symbol of inner power) and of healing. In kahuna psychology, Kanaloa represents the ideal person, fully aware, fully loving, filled with power, and fully at home in the spiritual and material worlds. Interestingly, *kanaloa* as a common word means "secure, firm, immovable, established, unconquerable, and the very best." The more or less formal process for achieving this state is called *haipule* or the Ha Prayer.

### THE HA PRAYER

The Ha Prayer, *haipule*, refers to a general process rather than to one specific ritual. I will give you a particularly effective format to use, but the more you understand the process, the more effective the format will be.

As is usual with very important words in Huna, the roots of the word contain a great many meanings that explain the concept of the word as a whole. *Haipule* has the general meaning of "religious, devout, pious; a pious person; to make prayers or hold a service." *Ha* has a basic meaning of "breath, life, trough, or sluice," and also the number four. Now, part of the prayer process includes increasing *mana*, the life force, and one of the best and easiest ways to do this is by deep breathing. The meaning of trough or sluice indicates that both the breathing and the whole process act as a channel for the intent of the prayer. Four is a sacred number in Huna; it symbolizes life, activity and manifestation.

*Hai* has the meaning of "to accompany, to go with," and *pu* also has the additional meaning of "together with," both of which refer to joining the three selves as part of the prayer process. This is emphasized again by the fact that *le'a* means to complete something successfully, and also refers to a type of prayer made to Kane, Ku, and Lono, code names for the three selves.

*Haipule*, then, can be described from the roots as a process in which you channel *mana* into yourself by breathing (or some other method) and send it forth to manifest something.

Now let's take a closer look at *mana* and how it works in Huna prayer.

### MANA IN THOUGHT AND ACTION

*Mana*, the energy of creation, is also the power of authority, which refers to unquestioning belief in one's ability or right to make something happen or be accepted. *Authority* interestingly, comes from the word *author*, which comes from a Latin word meaning "to originate, to create, creator." To make it simple, we can say that *mana* is the power of belief and the power to create. Even more simply, we can think of it as pure energy.

There is a Huna aphorism which says, "Energy flows where attention goes." Wherever you put your attention —on a thought, an object, an experience—a current of energy is generated between you and it. The more focused your attention is, the more free from distraction or resistance, the stronger the current. The primary causes of resistance are doubt and fear. If you increase the amount of *mana*, which is equivalent to increasing the voltage, you strengthen the current to the point where it can flow right through the resistance. We have seen how *mana* can be increased by numerous breathing and visualization exercises, as well as by physical means. However, this often produces side effects such as a temporary magnification of the resistance, which may completely distract the attention.

A second way to strengthen the current, requiring an increase in *mana*, is to remove the resistances. This means removing the fears and doubts. Once these are gone, the manifestation of your aim takes place without effort. Whatever you do well and easily now, you do because you have no fear or doubt about it. You just put your attention on it and you do it or it happens. Existing fears and doubts are not so easily removed, though, and ordinarily it requires a great deal of persistence and repetition of new ideas or practices before it takes place, as already discussed.

A third way, one that will be presented here, is to raise the frequency of the energy. This is like sitting in your living room watching a show that fills you with fear and doubt on a regular TV channel, and then switching to a UHF channel with a program that fills you with happiness and inspiration. It is the same you and the same living room, but the higher frequency lifted you right out of the place where fear and doubt exist.

In terms of personal *mana*, higher frequencies are represented by "higher" thoughts. I am not speaking of positive thinking but higher thinking, spiritual thinking. Spiritual thinking involves a totally different view of the world and your life, an attitude of loving trust toward your body, your subconscious, your High Self, the earth, the universe, and God. By filling your mind with spiritual thoughts, you can transcend fear and doubt without having to fight them, and you can achieve your aims more easily and enjoyably.

If you also increase your *mana* at this higher frequency level, then the results can be spectacular. What it takes, though, is constant remembering until the new level is established as a habit. While you are there, things work beautifully, but it is easy to forget and slip back into the ordinary world where most people still live. However, it doesn't take effort, just remembering. When you forget, and fear and doubt begin to have their effects again, simply remember, and those effects will disappear.

### PREPARATION FOR HAIPULE

This inner preparation is intended to make the *haipule* more effective, and it is represented by four Hawaiian words, *ike, kala, makia,* and *manawa.*

With a basic meaning of "awareness," *ike* in this context serves as a reminder to be aware of the existence of your three selves as a first step in integration. In fact, that is what the preparation is all about. Practically speaking, start out by being aware of your subconscious as the mind of your body, your friend and companion in life. At the very least, be aware of your body as yours and accept it in the here and now as lovingly as you can. Then be aware of your conscious mind, or intellect if you will, and be aware that this part of your mind can look outward or inward and focus on anything you will it to. Next, be aware of your High Self or God as a presence within and around you, as life, existence, and awareness itself. Finally, be aware that these three are intimately part of one another, and your very attempt at such awareness will increase the contact. When I say "be aware," that can mean thinking the thought, using your imagination, or having a feeling.

Relaxing your muscles is part of *kala* and so is calming your emotions (the two go hand in hand), but the word also means "to forgive," and that is an important part of the preparation. As best you can, clear your mind of guilt and resentments. One way is to remove all the "shoulds" from your memories, and another is to purposely praise yourself for whatever you did right in the situations you feel guilty about, and praise whatever is good about the people you feel resentment toward. Although you may not feel like doing this at first, remember that guilt and resentment are almost as much obstacles to your aim as fear and doubt.

*Makia* means "to concentrate," and this step involves deciding what your aim really is. I am not speaking here of a specific goal but of a purpose, something that will give meaning to your whole life. In the way I use the terms, goals are measures of progress in achieving your purpose. For instance, if your purpose or aim is to achieve enlightenment in this lifetime, then specific goals might include freeing your mind from limiting beliefs and mastering various forms of meditation. Each limiting belief removed and each meditation performed would be goals accomplished that serve your purpose. If your purpose or aim is to master wealth, then specific goals might include gaining certain knowledge and skills, accumulating certain amounts of money, and accomplishing certain projects. The attainment of knowledge, skills, money, and accomplishments would measure your progress in your purpose. Unlike a goal, a purpose is not something you reach but something you do. Goals without a purpose make for a life empty of meaning, while having a purpose can give meaning to any goal. For many people the most practical way to start

161

is to decide that your aim is to find a worthy purpose.

One translation of the roots for *manawa* is "power-time." That time of power, your time of power, is *NOW*. As part of the preparation for *haipule*, this means to bring your thoughts, your feelings, and your senses into the present moment, and purposely leaving the past and future alone. This is the most effective kind of centering, grounding, or whatever you choose to call it.

Easy ways to stay in the present are to notice the colors and shapes of things in your immediate environment, listen to the sounds around you, and pay attention to the sensations of your body, all without interpretations or analysis. For some people this may be difficult at first, but it is a delightful experience when you get used to it. Actually, it is when you are focused in the present moment that you are most effective at whatever you do, including creative and spiritual work. This is because your *mana* exists in this moment of consciousness and nowhere else.

As an aid to remembering the preparation process, you can memorize and recite the following related Huna aphorisms, while carrying on the appropriate activity in your mind:

> *Ike*—I (the three of me) create my own reality;
>
> *Kala*—I am unlimited;
>
> *Makia*—I get what I concentrate on;
>
> *Manawa*—My moment of power is now.

#### DOING HAIPULE

In doing *haipule* you are creating a state in which things can happen naturally. You are not trying to make them or force them to happen. You are not even asking for them to happen. It is not "prayer" in the Western sense at all, which really means "to entreat, implore, request." In Hawaiian this is *koi* or *noi*.

*Haipule* has nothing to do with offerings and sacrifice, an idea which is actually alien to the kahuna way of thinking as it is based on an idea that God can or has to be bribed or paid in order to do something for you. Unfortunately, this fearborn superstition has been used from ancient times to the present as a way for religious leaders to control their faithful and create an income at the same time. There is nothing wrong with supporting a religious leader as long as you realize that's what you are doing. What the early missionaries translated as "offering, sacrifice," was, in the minds of the kahunas, "planting seeds to grow and increase." There is a world of difference in intent and result between bribery or payment and sowing seed for a harvest. For the kahunas, thought and action are the seeds, and *mana* is what makes them strong and fertile.

*Pule* is not prayer. It is more like contemplation, "expectantly keeping your mind on something," with the added Huna understanding that whatever you contemplate, without doubt, will manifest in the nearest possible way. When you focus your attention on something with open expectation, vibrations stirred up by your thought go forth and either draw the equivalent experience to you (or you to it), or set in motion forces that create what wasn't there before. Even desire and wanting can get in the way of this process if they imply or evoke any idea of doubt at all. In the state of *haipule* you are together with your thought/image/feeling in the present moment. That, in essence, is spiritual integration.

*Haipule* can be done anywhere, any time, and under any circumstances, but the more undistracted your attention is, the better the results will be. I recommend setting aside a quiet time and place, if you can, for a more formal process, and I also recommend informal practice in the course of your daily activities. *Haipule* can be done in a minute or an hour; it's up to you.

After your preparation, begin focusing your attention on the areas given below, one by one. First think of the word, then think of a situation, condition, or person that best represents the meaning of that word to you

163

(imagine it with as much sensory detail as you can), and finally, get a feeling to go along with the word and the image. The feeling is very important, so choose an image that is most likely to produce a good feeling. If you are concerned about what feeling to have, use happiness.

The words are:

> *Peace (maluhia)*. Think of scenes of quiet beauty, like deep forests, open meadows, sunrises and sunsets; or scenes of people ceasing to fight and reaching out to hug; or whatever idea the word evokes in you.
>
> *Love (aloha)*. Think of children playing happily together; of being held and cuddled by someone who really loves you; of people doing great and daring things for each other with no thought of return; of scenes of acceptance, caring, forgiving; of anything else the word evokes in you.
>
> *Power (mana)*. Think of the power of God in nature, of suns and stars, of rivers and waterfalls, of all the energy of fire, earth, air, and water; and whatever else the word means to you (but not control over people).
>
> *Success (pono)*. Think of scenes that represent your highest ideals of achievement; of the attainment of important goals; of joyful accomplishment of any kind. (These may be "spiritual" or "material." In Huna there is no distinction when it is done with a loving attitude).

When you have finished with each word, you can end with an image/feeling of gratitude toward your High Self or God, and a blessing of some kind for the good of others. Then simply take a deep breath, open your eyes, and come back to the outer present, still concentrating in the now.

### RESULTS OF HAIPULE

I know that *haipule* in this form will seem too simple for many people. It is true that the kahunas would often add more or less elaborate ritual and ceremony to the process, with sacred objects and special clothing.

But all that was to impress the subconscious of the participants or to help focus concentration. I have given the essence of what was done in effective *haipule* regardless of the outer show, and you can dress it up in any way you choose. Just remember that the effectiveness comes from holding the undoubting thought, and from nothing else. Positive emotion, when you use it, serves mainly to raise you into that realm of absolute conviction.

How often should you practice? All the time, if you can, formally or informally, as much as you can. To be the way you want to be, you have to *think* the way you want to be. If no doubt gets in the way, one *haipule* can be enough. If doubt already exists as a habit, then a thousand a day won't be too much.

What can you expect? Ordinarily, you will gradually become more peaceful, more loving, more powerful, and more successful in every way, without a lot of effort. You will still have to make choices and act on opportunities that appear, but the struggle will fade away and your happiness and joy will increase and grow.

Now you are equipped with ideas, tools, and techniques that will enable you to resolve any problem and reach any goal. You know about the Huna concept of three selves and how they interrelate with each other, the physical body, and the world. You know about *aka* and *mana* and their part in the creation of personal experience. You know how to clear negative complexes, guide and direct your subconscious, make better use of your conscious mind, and contact your High Self. You have learned ways of using dreams, your personal energy, and various forms of meditation for enhancing your life. And you have learned how to integrate the natural abilities of your three selves with the process of *haipule*.

Let's pay particular attention to that last point, integration. You can resolve many problems in your life by working with your subconscious alone. You can accomplish many goals with just the driving force of your conscious will. And you can reach states of incredible bliss by focusing strictly on your High Self. But you won't be complete—you won't *feel* complete—unless all three of your selves have a harmonious relationship, unless all three are recognized, respected, and reconciled.

Knowing what you know is not enough. The next and vital step is to apply it. And that involves the part of you referred to in the title of this book. It is not your subconscious self that is hidden. Its presence is revealed in your body and behavior. It is not your High Self that is hidden, either, because its presence is revealed in your manifested experience. You have undoubtedly guessed by now that the self which is hidden, the one to master, is the self you know as *you*.

> E lawe i ke a'o a malama, a e 'oi mau ka na'auao. (He who takes his teachings and applies them increases his knowledge.)
>
> A Hawaiian proverb

# Appendix:
## THE SECRET CODE OF THE KAHUNAS

To say that there was a secret code hidden within the Hawaiian language is to imply that the language itself was artificially made. This concept is not without precedent. Esperanto, the language that was constructed for world use, is now used by speakers all over the world, as well as in libraries, newspapers, and radio stations. And some linguists are convinced that Arabic was purposely constructed on a mathematical basis.

As for Hawaiian, there is no real proof that it was artificially made, but there are some intriguing indications. One way in which linguists determine the length of time that languages have been in use is by their degree of simplicity. Contrary to what you might expect, the newer a language, the more complicated its grammar, while the older it is the more simple its construction. Hawaiian is so simple that it doesn't use the verb *to be*, has no separate words for *past, present,* and *future,* uses only twelve letters, and yet it is capable of adaptation to any modern concepts. This is either an extremely ancient language or one made deliberately. Another indication, of course, is the way the roots describe so accurately the knowledge of Huna.

### THE CODE LANGUAGE

The code language, said to be designed by initiates to communicate Huna, is made up of simple roots which, when analyzed, explain some aspect of Huna. Kahunas hold that in order to provide greater flexibility, several meanings were often given to the roots and compound words and that, as the language grew in use, extended meanings were sometimes added that had nothing to do with Huna. Symbolic meanings were included for both security and greater flexibility in transmission. For instance, *mana*, "divine power," was symbolized by water and fire, and *aka*, "etheric substance," by clusters of fruit or a shining star, to name only a few.

Let us look at the word *mana* in terms of the code language. By itself, the word means supernatural or divine power, miraculous power of any kind, power in general, authority, privilege. The word *power* in this context includes the concepts of energy, confidence, and skill. Other meanings for *mana* are "to branch out or spread out" and "arid, desert." Though seemingly unrelated, those meanings actually describe effects of the mysterious energy that is *mana* and the effects of having or losing confidence. In the following examination of roots, we will concentrate on the energy aspect of *mana*. This energy has also been called *life force, prana,* and *orgone.*

To get at the root meanings, we first break the word into syllables. *Ma* has a code meaning of "by means of," indicating that certain things are done by means of *mana*. *Ma* also means "to fade away," and *mana* can indeed fade away under certain circumstances. The same syllable is used for the shortened form of the word for eye and for desire. The physical eyes emit *mana*, and *mana* is necessary for obtaining desires. The syllable *na* means "calmed, quieted, pacified," which describes the state of a person full of *mana* (*ma* is also a common prefix indicating a quality or state, so *ma-na* can mean "a state of peace"). Another meaning of *na* is "to relieve pain," a major characteristic of *mana*.

Other code meanings can be derived from doubling the syllables. *Mama* means "fast, speedy, nimble of movement," a good description of the action of *mana*. Also, "light of weight" and "eased of pain, ache or distress," more descriptions of *mana* and its effects. Interestingly, the compound words *eamama* and *akemama* mean "oxygen" and "lungs" respectively. Taking oxygen into the lungs is one of the principal ways in which *mana* is accumulated. *Nana* has the meanings of "to pay attention to" and "to take care of," both of which are important in regard to *mana*.

It is not enough to simply use the apparent syllables to get at all the code meanings in a word. The ancient Hawaiians loved word games and they must be played in order to get at complete meanings. For a simple word like *mana*, the only word game consists in dropping the *m* to get *ana*, which means "a pattern, plan, or model" and "satisfied." In learning how to use and direct *mana*, one channels it into a mental pattern or model, and the result, of course, is satisfaction. A doubling of this syllable, *ana-ana*, basically means "excessively patterned" to the point of causing limitations, and it is the Hawaiian word for black magic.

Finally, you can double the vowels. *Ma'a* means "knowing thoroughly, to practice, to gain skill or develop a habit," all of which are uses to which *mana* can be put. And *na'a* means "firmly seated," a reference to the confidence associated with *mana*.

This is basically the process by which words are broken down in Hawaiian to find code meanings which explain particular concepts more fully. By using our intuition through this technique, we now know much more about *mana* than the fact that it means divine power. As its root meanings are compared to those of other code words, even more clarification is achieved. Understanding of the root meanings becomes even clearer with a comparison to the known practices of the kahunas, plus a general knowledge of psychoreligious systems in the rest of the world.

#### POLYNESIAN IN GREECE

Abraham Fornander, a nineteenth century resident of Hawaii, did extensive linguistic and cultural studies in an attempt to prove that the original homeland of the Polynesians was in the Near East. Max Freedom Long was also convinced of this and claimed to have received confirmation for the idea from a man who lived with a Berber tribe in North Africa. Today most anthropologists hold the opinion that the Polynesians came from India or Southeast Asia and a few, like Thor Heyerdahl, tend toward a South American origin.

However, the kahunas of Hawaii claim that their knowledge and culture originated in the Pacific and spread from there to the rest of the world. This idea gets support from an unexpected and unintended source. In 1969, John Philip Cohane, a writer and student of archeology, was doing some research on the Irish and became amazed at the reoccurrence of certain key words and place names. More research revealed the repetition of these same key words all over the world. In his book on this research, *The Key*, Cohane strongly suggests that the worldwide distribution of these words was due to ancient Semitic migrations, but in the light of the kahuna tradition another interpretation is possible. From Cohane's book I would like to quote these very intriguing paragraphs:

> Moving westward across the Pacific Ocean from the Peruvian coast, hopping from island to island all the way to and including China and the rest of the Asian mainland, the impact of the same key names is

170

overwhelming, far greater than it has been anywhere else . . . The identical combinations appear again and again on islands separated from one another by thousands of miles of open ocean.

In Hawaii one finds: . . . Aloha: the word or name extended both as a welcome and a farewell, identical phonetically to Eloah, the Semitic name for God. With a global relationship growing stronger, Alloa, the oldest recorded greeting in the British Isles, the forerunner of Hello, commands more attention.

Hula: the name of the celebrated native dance, accepted as coming from a religious origin with strong fertility overtones, is a common variant of Eloah/Allah/Ala in place-names. In addition to a number of Ula names, some already mentioned, note Hula in Ethiopia, El Hula in Lebanon, Lake Hula in Israel, the Hulahula River in Alaska, Hulah Reservoir in Oklahoma, as well as Mount Huila and Huila Division in Colombia, a name which appears twice in Angola, Africa.

It is possible that some of these names, and the hundreds of others that Cohane has noted, are merely due to coincidental similarities of language sounds, but they do lead to the speculation of a worldwide distribution of Polynesian place names. The notion that these similarities are due to the cultural impact of ancient voyagers from the Pacific is reinforced by a Huna researcher in California who discovered that the code language of the kahunas may have been known and used in and around early Greece.

An article in *Time* magazine, dated February 28, 1972, described an archeological expedition to the tiny island of Santorini in the Aegean Sea. The expedition was looking for traces of Atlantis, but that does not concern us here. What does concern us are the names of two volcanoes on the island, Nea Kameni and Palaia Kameni. It should also be noted that Santorini boasted a highly civilized society before it was destroyed in 1500 B.C. by a devastating volcanic explosion.

The mere fact that the names of the volcanoes sound

somewhat like Hawaiian does not mean anything, except that it provided the first clue. In Greek, the two names merely mean "New Furnace" and "Old Furnace," but if there is any real correlation to the Huna tradition we should be able to examine the roots of the volcano names and find correspondences in Hawaiian.

In Hawaiian, *nea* means "empty, bare, desolated" and "to lay waste or make destitute." Further meanings are "volcanic cinder or pumice." There is no Hawaiian word like *kameni* except a word derived from English to mean "cement," but from *ka* we get "to fling or hurl," "to curse," and "to go out from the center." The doubling, *kaka*, means "odorous." The roots *a me* and *me* only mean "and" and "with." *Ni*, which we have to change into *nia* to conform to Hawaiian grammar, means "to remove all vestige of vegetation." *Pa* (from Palaia) means "a sound" and "parched land." *Papa'a*, a doubling of both syllable and vowel which is used in the code, means "to burn or scorch." "To smear or smudge" is a meaning of *pala*, while *ala* means "dense, waterworn volcanic stone." *La* means "heat" and *la'a* means "doomed to death or destruction." *Ai* has the meanings of "to destroy or consume, as by fire" and *aia* means "wickedness."

From all of the above we get a very good picture of volcanoes and their effects, which stretches any idea of coincidence out of shape. But is it proof of kahuna influence? Some people will accept hearsay as proof and others will resist changing their ideas whatever the weight of evidence. You must make your own choice. However, the article with its map is available and you may want to check it out with your own dictionary. There is no test better than personal experience.

### CULTURAL CORRELATIONS

Other than direct translations of place names, one of the ways of correlating Huna to the systems of thought in various areas of the world is to study the cultural concepts of the latter and see whether the Huna code displays similar ideas.

Sufism, for instance, is a form of mysticism associated with Islam, but which claims an existence which predates Christianity. There is a Sufi legend that tells of an island to which people fled when their own land became uninhabitable. Later, it was safe to go back, but by then most of the people had forgotten how good their former land was and wanted to stay where they were. A few people learned to swim and reached their former land to find it wonderful beyond compare. They came back to teach others how to swim, but most of the rest did not want to learn, and those that did wanted to learn without all the training. In brief, the legend is meant to convey the idea of man having fallen from a better state and losing his knowledge of his true self, and of the difficulty faced by those who have acquired the knowledge in passing it on to others.

Now a correlation to Polynesian legends would take up too much space, but it might be interesting enough to look at a couple of key words. *Moku,* Hawaiian for "island," also means "to be cut off, separated, to be bound in one place." *Au*, a word for "self" and "thought," has additional meanings of "to swim, to learn to swim, to teach to swim." Again, not proof, but a very nice coincidence.

Max Freedom Long translated the Lord's Prayer into Hawaiian, then into the code language, and back into English. In this way he found that it contains an explicit instruction for making contact with one's Higher Self. It is not just a prayer to be repeated, but a formula for achieving results. Throughout the New Testament the formula is repeated in various ways, as if to make certain the initiated reader would not miss it. No doubt there was also the realization that some parts of the writings might be cut and whole books might even disappear.

I, myself, have found that there is a tremendous

amount of very clear and open correlation between most of the Gospel teachings and Huna. For instance, over and over again the statement is made to those who have received a healing: "Thy faith hath made thee whole." This is a direct equivalent of the Huna teaching that healing is caused by a change in belief. Such a correlation alone wouldn't mean much, but I have found a multitude of similar instances for each of the basic principles of Huna.

As for the Old Testament, the Huna teachings are found there, too, clothed in the meanings of personal and place names. This was a favorite way to pass on knowledge of both the ancient kahunas and the ancient Hebrew writers. The outer story would serve mainly as a carrier for the real information hidden in the names. You must understand, of course, that the Bible, like many other sacred books, has a multitude of meanings. The fact that Huna meanings are found in it does not eliminate the possibility of other hidden meanings being present, or even that the outer meanings have no value. In the modern West we no longer expect several layers of meaning written into the same text. Few writers practice the technique, and few readers are capable of appreciating it. Even the original sociopolitical meanings of Mother Goose rhymes are lost to the majority of people today.

The ancient kahunas were experts at building multiple layers of meaning into chants and songs. Take the following chant recorded in *The Kahunas* by L. R. McBride:

> Remember the days of our youth
> Swollen now are the clouds of Hanakahi
> Swelled now above the eyes is the cloud
>    of morning
> In vain is the battle of children
> The great battle will follow
> As the deep sea follows shallow water
> The warrior arises
> Ready alike for victory and defeat.

This chant may contain as many as five different meanings—literal, figurative, sexual, historical, and a secret meaning only for the initiates.

If the writers of the Bible were initiates into the ancient teachings found in Huna, they would have no trouble doing the same thing. As a matter of fact, whether they were initiates or not, they did use multiple layers of meaning. To use just one example, the story of the Garden of Eden has a layer of meaning hidden in the place names which describes the process for maintaining a high mental state of prosperity and happiness, and the effects that occur when you allow negative thinking to take over. *Gan-Heden,* "the Garden of Eden" in Hebrew, is a state of consciousness, not simply a physical location on the earth.

## WHY SO SECRET?

Why was it necessary to have a secret code? Why was it necessary to keep Huna from the general community? The first reason that usually comes to mind is that of maintaining a position of power. The theory goes that a few people discovered secrets of great value like telepathy and psychokinesis and decided not to tell anyone else so that they could rule without rivals. Unfortunately, this theory is based on an attitude of "sour grapes." It is only when real power begins to be lost that those who are supposed to have the power resort to secrecy for this reason. They feel forced to hide the fact of the loss from the people, and the false secrecy they promote can keep people ignorant of the truth for a long time. In fact, they are at pains to advertise the fact that they *have* a secret, because who would know it otherwise? This was the case with the kahunas of the island of Molokai at about the time of Captain Cook's arrival in the Hawaiian Islands. They had a reputation of being terrible and powerful sorcerers. When King Kamehameha conquered the island, however, he found that all they had was a reputation.

Another theory has it that the great secrets are kept so as to prevent them from being used for evil purposes. This is about as effective as was the United States' intention to keep the process of atomic energy a secret. The secrets of life cannot be kept from those with black hearts who are intelligent enough to understand them and ambitious enough to apply them. The only saving factor is that the very greatest secrets require a loving heart to be used. Nevertheless, there is a whole range of knowledge that can be used equally for good or harm, which is why some kahunas specialize in counteracting evil.

There are two valid principal reasons for keeping the secrets of life secret. One is the danger of persecution. The true secrets of life usually do not conform to the beliefs of those in power, whose powers rest on the maintenance of those beliefs. This applies whether we are talking about religious, political, or scientific authorities, for the true secrets of life tend to make people more independent of any earthly authority.

The second reason is the difficulty of imparting the secrets. Understanding them often requires a complete change of thinking on the part of the aspirant, something few people are willing to undertake. Most people are basically lazy. They either want the moon without any effort, or they want to achieve miracles without undergoing the necessary inner transformation. Now it is well to note that many of the secrets can be experienced easily. The real difficulty lies in living according to the principles that they imply and in practicing to improve skill.

# Index

**Quest Books**
encourages open-minded inquiry into
world religions, philosophy, science, and the arts
in order to understand the wisdom of the ages,
respect the unity of all life, and help people explore
individual spiritual self-transformation.

Its publications are generously supported by
The Kern Foundation,
a trust committed to Theosophical education.

Quest Books is the imprint of
the Theosophical Publishing House,
a division of the Theosophical Society in America.
For information about programs, literature,
on-line study, membership benefits, and international centers,
see www.theosophical.org
or call 800-669-1571 or (outside the U.S.) 630-668-1571.

**Related Quest Titles**

*Earth Energies,* by Serge King

*Kahuna Healing,* by Serge King

*The Road to Self-Mastery* (CD), by Serge King

To order books or a complete Quest catalog,
call 800-669-9425 or (outside the U.S.) 630-665-0130.